THE METHODS
COACH

Learning Through Practice

THE METHODS
COACH

Learning Through Practice

Lance W. Roberts   **Karen Kampen**   **Tracey Peter**

OXFORD
UNIVERSITY PRESS

OXFORD
UNIVERSITY PRESS

70 Wynford Drive, Don Mills, Ontario M3C 1J9
www.oupcanada.com

Oxford University Press is a department of the University of Oxford.
It furthers the University's objective of excellence in research, scholarship,
and education by publishing worldwide in

Oxford   New York

Auckland   Cape Town   Dar es Salaam   Hong Kong   Karachi
Kuala Lumpur   Madrid   Melbourne   Mexico City   Nairobi
New Delhi   Shanghai   Taipei   Toronto

With offices in

Argentina   Austria   Brazil   Chile   Czech Republic   France   Greece
Guatemala   Hungary   Italy   Japan   Poland   Portugal   Singapore
South Korea   Switzerland   Thailand   Turkey   Ukraine   Vietnam

Oxford is a trade mark of Oxford University Press
in the UK and in certain other countries

Published in Canada
by Oxford University Press

Library and Archives Canada Cataloguing in Publication

Roberts, Lance W., 1950–
The methods coach : learning through practice / Lance Roberts,
Karen Kampen & Tracey Peter.

Includes index.
ISBN 978-0-19-542658-8

1. Research—Methodology—Textbooks. I. Kampen, Karen
II. Peter, Tracey, 1973– III. Title.

Q180.55.M4R62 2009   001.4'2   C2008-906174-9

Cover image: ImageSource Photography/Veer

This book is printed on permanent acid-free paper.
Printed and bound in Canada.

1 2 3 4 — 12 11 10 09

Table of Contents

'You Play the Way You Practise': A Preface for Students

The Importance of Practise

Athletic coaches drill their players with the dictum 'You play the way you practise.' This aphorism applies to all endeavours in which 'knowing' and 'doing' must be bridged. It is one thing to 'talk a good game' but quite another to master the challenges of performance. In connecting knowing with doing, practice is the key—whether in sports, in the kitchen, or in the classroom.

This book is intended to give you an opportunity to 'practise' several of the fundamental concepts and principles you are learning in your research methods course. Contrary to popular belief, practice does *not* make perfect. What practice does is *habituate*. If you repeatedly swing a golf club incorrectly or overcook your pasta, then you will surely habituate these performance deficiencies.

Learning through Coaching

For practice to be useful in improving your performance, it is optimal if you have a 'coach'. For learning, the role of a coach has two important components, one of which occurs prior to practice and the other after practice.

Prior to practice, a coach needs to *raise your awareness* of critical performance features. In the case of a golf swing, this might include noting your grip, club take-away, or position at the top of the swing. In the case of pasta preparation, it might mean the temperature of the water, ingredients added to it, or cooking time. In any case, raising your awareness alerts you to key things to keep in mind when you practise.

After you have performed, the coach plays a second key role: to *provide you with constructive feedback*. The goal of feedback is to let you see how you have performed compared to a preferred standard. You thought your golf swing was slow and smooth, but your coach tells you that it was actually quick and jerky. You thought you put enough oil into the water and took the pasta out in time, but you did neither—resulting in a sticky mass of starch.

In short, an optimal performance learning strategy involves three components. First, you are made aware of the key requirements of the skill. Second, you make the effort to perform the skill. Finally, you receive constructive feedback about your performance.

The Model

This text is based on the three-component 'coaching' model. It implements the model in the form of 'labs' familiar to students in the natural sciences like chemistry and biology. A lab is a place of practice that is preceded by a 'demonstration' (that alerts students to key performance features) and followed by 'feedback' (on the lab report based upon student performance).

The book contains 12 methods labs. Each lab consists of three parts: a 'tune-up', a 'lab application', and 'constructive feedback', which work as follows:

- *The tune-up*: Each module begins with a tune-up giving you a succinct overview of the central methodological concepts that are the focus of the lab. The intention of this component is to review and highlight the core concepts under consideration.
- *The lab application*: After the tune-up has focused your thinking, the lab gives you the opportunity to solidify your understanding of the core concepts through application. These applications aim at realism in presenting challenges similar to those faced by practising social researchers.
- *Constructive feedback*: The first two steps of each lab clarify core concepts and provide you with guided opportunities to put these ideas into practice. The final step involves feedback. Immediate, constructive feedback is necessary for reinforcement and remediation. The website associated with this book (www.oupcanada.com/methodscoach) provides feedback in a section available through your instructor. It includes answers to the application questions and identifies and clarifies the most common forms of misapplication.

What's Covered

This book is not intended to replace the textbook used in your course. Rather, it supplements your textbook in that it helps to solidify your understanding of key methodological concepts and principles through guided application.

Any good-quality methods text covers a much larger range of topics than the ones we focus on in this book. Of necessity, your textbook provides an overview of many topics, while the 12 labs in this volume focus more intensely on key methodological concepts and principles.[1] The goal is to move you from the basic understanding you will derive from your textbook to a more thorough understanding informed through practice.

The methods labs cover the following key topics:

Lab 1   The building blocks: Variables and hypotheses
Lab 2   Errors in reasoning
Lab 3   Conceptual and operational definitions
Lab 4   Levels of measurement
Lab 5   Quantitative sampling considerations

Developing Confidence

Genuine self-confidence and self-esteem[2] are precious (perhaps *the most* precious) human qualities. Authentic self-confidence and associated self-esteem derive from the *mastery* of something *worthwhile* and *difficult*. This is why these precious commodities are not awarded for incompetence (versus mastery), frivolousness (versus worth), or simplicity (versus difficulty).

For this reason, we have deliberately offered ideas and applications that you should find challenging. If you do, this is a positive sign, because if you are not moved out of your comfort zone, you will not grow.

Learning is different from certification. Learning involves change, and change inevitably involves making errors. So don't be afraid to make mistakes. And, just as important, don't let your mistakes discourage you.

We encourage you to study the tune-up points carefully and put forward your best effort in each lab application. If you get stuck while working on an application, consult the 'Tips for lab applications' section on the companion website (www.oupcanada.com/methodscoach). It does not provide answers or solutions but rather hints about how you should proceed. The tips cover steps where experience has shown students commonly get stuck. They are meant to give you a 'push' that moves you along when you get bogged down.

Through your instructor, you can gain access to the model answers we have constructed for the application questions. Using this feedback on your completed assignment, you will learn something—either that you can successfully put the ideas into practice or that your skills need refining. When you learn that you have succeeded, your confidence will deservedly grow. When you learn that your skills need more work, that should motivate you to return to the core ideas and continue your informed practice. The path to success and confidence is through successive approximations.

Share Your Experience

Our students have benefited greatly from each of the lab applications presented in this book. However, we are practitioners of what we preach and are certain that improvements can be made. If you would like to share your experience in working through the labs or have constructive suggestions for improvement, please send them along to Lance_Roberts@umanitoba.ca.

We trust that you will learn as much from working with these applications as we did from producing them.

Lance W. Roberts
Karen Kampen
Tracey Peter

LAB 1
The Building Blocks: Variables and Hypotheses

◗ Tune-up

Variables and hypotheses are the building blocks of research. The following tune-up section supplements your course readings and provides a review of some of the principal points you will need to understand in order to answer the lab questions related to these fundamentals.

Human interest in difference and change

A wealthy member of the European nobility regularly hosts dinner parties at his estate in Switzerland, which is situated on a beautiful lake, surrounded by mountain views. The vista from the stone veranda is stunning and picture-perfect. During the cocktail hour preceding the dinner, guests who look out into the distance on the lake see a small figure rowing a boat back and forth between two points of shoreline. The rower's presence is no accident, nor is the fact that he is a more routine topic of conversation than the spectacular landscape.

What the noble estate-owner learned from experience is that after its initial stunning impact, the spectacular view from the veranda does little to capture his guests' attention. And consequently, it does not serve as a source of conversation among guests who arrive as strangers. The rower, however, does capture their attention, again and again, as he rows his way from point to point. That is why the host pays him to perform during the cocktail hour. He is an 'ice-breaker'.

This story illustrates a fundamental fact of human experience: *what interests us is change, diversity, or difference.* You see this fact in operation wherever you look. From conversations between friends over coffee, to reports on the evening television news, to intelligence briefings provided by spy agencies, we attend to and are interested in what has changed, what is different.

The research interest in variables

'Research' literally means 'to look again', and *one important driver of the research act is an interest in change, diversity, and difference.* In this way, the researcher is similar to the dinner guests in the Swiss Alps.

Researchers capture their interest in 'differences' by translating them into tools called 'variables'. Variables are the working stuff of most research. Textbooks and dictionaries provide slightly different definitions of the term, but at root, variables can be viewed as *properties of objects that can change.* In the case of the rower on the lake, it is his position on the lake that is variable (and consequently of interest). The attention of researchers in different disciplines is captured by different changing properties, by different forms of diversity. As selected illustrations, consider the astronomer's interest in the motion of the planets, the sociologist's in income inequalities, the military historian's in propensity for war, or the psychologist's in intelligence differences.

By the way, *the opposite of a variable is a 'constant'*, which is a property of an object that does *not* change. Constants are fixed and, like the nobleman's unchanging vista, are generally less interesting than variables.

The components of variables

Variables draw our attention to diversity, difference, or change. For example, 'social class' qualifies as a variable because different people belong to different social classes (diversity), different nations have different sizes of middle-class (difference), or the distribution of social classes in a society changes over time.

If variables capture change, then the *change must be evident across some categories.* These categories comprise the 'components' of variables. For example, the variable 'social class' may be comprised of upper-, middle-, and lower-class categories, 'gender' as male and female, 'income' as differing dollar amounts earned.

The categories that are the components of a variable are identified by different names. You may see them called *attributes, scores, or values.* Whatever the label, these classifications *capture the range of differences* across which the variable can change.

Criteria for adequate variables

Variables are the tools researchers use to capture change, difference, or diversity in some property among objects being observed or measured. By using variables, researchers intend to distinguish objects in terms of the property under consideration. Identifying the differences between objects with respect to some property requires two things. First, all objects need to be measured in terms of the variable, and second, all objects need to have only a single score on the variable.

Technically, these two properties of adequate variables are labelled 'exhaustiveness' and 'mutual exclusiveness'. When a variable is 'exhaustive', it means that its *attributes include all of the possible scores that might be observed* (its scores 'exhaust' the possibilities). When a variable meets the criterion of 'mutual exclusiveness', it means that the categories of the variable do not overlap.

Taken together, these two criteria for adequate variables mean that (i) every object can be measured in terms of the variable (exhaustiveness) and (ii) every object can receive only one score on the variable (mutual exclusiveness).

Accounting for differences

Variables capture our interest and are routinely followed by the explanatory question 'why?' In short, we are curious about why the observed differences, diversity, or change captured by a variable exists. Why are some nations more likely to go to war than others? Why do some communities have higher crime rates than others? Why did Jean get a divorce?

The technique used to account for observed differences in a variable involves trying to *link these changes to changes in some other variable*. This notion is central to the explanatory approach using variables. In other words, researchers try to account for differences in a variable of interest by establishing a connection to changes in some other variable. Variables are used to explain other variables. Differences in education are used to explain differences in income; changes in diet are used to explain changes in body mass; ethnic diversity among nations is used to account for changing levels of social integration.

Types of variables

Researchers use different labels to distinguish between the variables whose differences are being explained and variables that are used to account for observed differences. The 'outcome' variable whose change originally captures our interest is labelled 'dependent', while the variable that is thought to 'produce' the change is called 'independent'. *In short, researchers try to account for differences in dependent variables by establishing linkages to changes in independent variables.*

Beyond the division between independent and dependent variables, researchers often use an additional distinction to classify variables. This additional classification distinguishes 'categorical' variables from 'numeric' variables. Whereas the independent/dependent variable distinction relates to the location of a variable in relationship to some other variable, the categorical/numeric distinction focuses on the nature of the variable's attributes.

Categorical (sometimes called 'discrete' or 'qualitative') variables are those whose attributes identify specific types or kinds of the variable being measured. In other words, the attributes of a categorical variable simply specify 'qualitative' (not quantitative) distinctions between the categories. Because the categories are qualitatively distinctive, they identify 'discrete' (i.e., separate) types of the variable being measured. Ethnicity is an example of a categorical variable. The attributes of the variable 'ethnicity' (e.g., Chinese, German, Irish, Ugandan) only indicate distinct types or qualities of ethnicity.

Numeric (sometimes called 'continuous' or 'quantitative') variables are those whose attributes can be numbered or rank-ordered. They are sometimes called 'continuous' variables because the ordered attributes of the variable flow from one to the next. Age is an example of a continuous variable. Different ages (i.e., attributes) do more than reflect different 'kinds' of age; these scores represent different 'amounts' of age.

Establishing relationships

Constructing a connection between independent and dependent variables essentially involves determining whether a relationship exists between the two variables. The term 'relationship' is evident when *a change in one variable is systematically related to a change in another variable*. The key here involves the word 'systematically'. Variables, by definition, change. Relationships do not exist simply because variables change. Instead, independent and dependent variables are 'related' when changes in the dependent (outcome) variable are *systematically connected* to changes in the independent (production) variable.

Hypotheses as predictions

Research is conducted to help fill gaps in our understanding, to help reduce our ignorance and increase our knowledge. After all, if we are confident that we know how some part of the world works, then we feel little need to research it. It is in areas where our understanding is uncertain that research is conducted. In such areas, predictions about what relationships we might expect to see between the independent and dependent variables of interest can assist us in our research ('looking again'). *These anticipated relationships between the independent and dependent variable are called 'hypotheses'.*

Sources of hypotheses

These expectations (i.e., hypotheses) about how some part of the world works (i.e., how independent and dependent variables are related) can come from a variety of sources. The sources of good ideas are multiple. Generally, however, researchers classify the sources of hypotheses as being either 'deductive' or 'inductive'.

Hypotheses are said to be deductive when they are derived from a theory. In other words, a deductive hypothesis is an expectation about a particular relationship between an independent and dependent variable that is *logically deduced from a general theory*. Inductive hypotheses, by contrast, express expected independent–dependent variable relationships that are *derived from observation or experience*. It is common to hear a hypothesis defined as an 'educated guess'. Deductive hypotheses derive their 'education' from theory, while inductive hypotheses derive theirs from experience.

Criteria for helpful hypotheses

A hypothesis serves as an expectation or a guide regarding what to expect when a relationship between independent and dependent variables is researched. The collection of evidence through research helps to determine whether the hypothetical prediction is more or less an adequate guide.

Hypotheses are more helpful as guides to research when they meet three criteria: clarity, directionality, and falsifiability. Clarity means that the independent and dependent variables are clearly identifiable. Directionality means that the character of the connection between the variables is specified. Falsifiability means that you can imagine evidence that would not support your hypothesis. A hypothesis becomes unclear when you cannot identify each of the variables predicted to be related. A hypothesis lacks directionality when it does not state how changes in one variable are related to changes in another. The common choices regarding directionality include 'positive' (which means that the variables change systematically in the *same direction*) and 'negative' (which means they change systematically in *opposite directions*). A hypothesis becomes unfalsifiable either when all evidence you can imagine collecting can be interpreted as supporting or confirming the prediction or when you cannot imagine evidence that would test the hypothesis.

LAB 1 APPLICATION

Learning objectives

The following lab questions are directed at helping you translate the tune-up points into concrete research situations. Specifically, this lab assignment challenges you to clarify your understanding of:

- the nature and components of variables;
- the distinction between independent and dependent variables;
- the qualities of helpful hypotheses;
- the derivation of deductive hypotheses.

Variables and their components

Identify whether each of the following terms is a variable or a constant. Justify your choices.

Size of city

Variable or constant? _____

Justification: _____

_____

_____

Sexual permissiveness

Variable or constant? _____

Justification: _____

_____

_____

Roman Catholic

Variable or constant? _____

Justification: _____

_____

_____

Religiosity

    Variable or constant? _____

    Justification: _____

    _____

    _____

Edmonton

    Variable or constant? _____

    Justification: _____

    _____

    _____

Marital happiness

    Variable or constant? _____

    Justification: _____

    _____

    _____

University graduate

    Variable or constant? _____

    Justification: _____

    _____

    _____

For each of the following variables, specify whether the attributes meet the criteria of mutual exclusiveness and exhaustiveness. If you see a problem, indicate what improvements are required to meet these criteria.

    Respondent's religion, using the following categories: Christian, Muslim, Jew, Catholic, Buddhist

        Mutually exclusive? _____ Exhaustive? _____

        Required improvements: _____

        _____

        _____

Respondent's age, using the following categories: 0–25 years, 25–30 years, 30–40 years, 40+ years

    Mutually exclusive? _____ Exhaustive? _____

    Required improvements: _____

    _____

    _____

Respondent's happiness, rated on a 7-point scale in which 1 = completely unhappy and 7 = completely happy

    Mutually exclusive? _____ Exhaustive? _____

Respondent's education level, using the following categories: less than high school, high school, technical/community college, some post-secondary, completed university degree

    Mutually exclusive? _____ Exhaustive? _____

    Required improvements: _____

    _____

    _____

Imagine that you are asked to develop a set of attributes for a variable that measures a respondent's occupation. In the space below, develop a set of mutually exclusive and exhaustive categories that would satisfy this task.

    Occupational categories:

    _____   _____

    _____   _____

    _____   _____

    _____   _____

Independent and dependent variables

For each of the following pairs of variables, which is the independent variable and which is the dependent variable? Make sure that you can justify your answers.

    Prevalence of lung cancer/Number of cigarettes smoked

        Independent variable: _____

        Justification: _____

Dependent variable: _____

Justification: _____

Number of hours studied/Final grade in introductory sociology

Independent variable: _____

Justification: _____

Dependent variable: _____

Justification: _____

Consumption of illegal drugs/Likelihood of dropping out of high school

Independent variable: _____

Justification: _____

Dependent variable: _____

Justification: _____

Identifying helpful hypotheses

Several research statements are listed below. Examine each statement to determine whether it meets the criteria of a helpful research hypothesis. If it does, then underneath the statement (i) identify the independent and dependent variables, and (ii) list at least two attributes of each variable. If the statement does not qualify as a helpful hypothesis, cross it out. Then underneath it (i) write a sentence explaining what was lacking or incorrect, and (ii) formulate an improved version.

Good students like to study at home more than at school.

_____

_____

_____

Race is positively related to socio-economic status.

_____

_____

_____

Level of education is positively related to personal income.

_____

_____

_____

A city's unemployment rate is negatively related to its population size.

_____

_____

_____

Sex is related to street crime.

_____

_____

_____

Protestants have higher suicide rates than Catholics do.

_____

_____

_____

One criterion of a good-quality hypothesis is falsifiability. Identify whether or not each of the following statements is falsifiable. Provide a one-sentence justification of your answer.

Weather forecast: Today there is a probability of precipitation.

_____

_____

Citizens of Canada enjoy more political freedom than those in Burma.

_____

_____

Alberta should share more of its oil wealth with the rest of Canada.

_____

_____

Middle-class couples experience lower divorce rates than lower-class couples do.

_____

_____

Below are three research scenarios. After reading each scenario, (i) identify the independent and dependent variables, and justify your choices; (ii) specify and justify whether each of the variables is categorical or numeric; and (iii) develop a good-quality hypothesis that relates the variables under consideration.

Scenario 1

Suppose that you have access to survey data suggesting that about half of the population who have never cohabited (i.e., lived common-law) would be willing to do so at some point, while the other half would not. You want to know why. Feminist theory tells you that in patriarchal societies, women enjoy much less sexual freedom than men do. Therefore, the normative proscription against non-marital sex imposes greater constraints on women than on men, and they suffer more serious consequences if they violate it. Your survey of 1,000 individuals has measured the variable *sex* (attributes: male, female) and *willingness to live common-law* (attributes: willing, unwilling).

Independent variable: _____

Justification: _____

_____

_____

Categorical or numeric: _____

Justification: _____

_____

_____

Dependent variable: _____

Justification: _____

_____

_____

Categorical or numeric: _____

Justification: _____

_____

_____

Hypothesis: _____

_____

_____

Scenario 2

You wonder why some people support the death penalty while others do not. Your survey has measured *level of support for the death penalty for murder* (on a scale of 1 to 5 in which 1 = totally opposed and 5 = totally in favour) and *age* (in years). Your reading of the available research literature indicates that as people grow older, their attitudes generally become more 'conservative'.

Independent variable: _____

Justification: _____

_____

_____

Categorical or numeric: _____

Justification: _____

_____

_____

Dependent variable: _____

Justification: _____

_____

_____

Categorical or numeric: _____

Justification: _____

_____

_____

Hypothesis: _____

_____

_____

Scenario 3

You notice that the personal incomes of students in your class vary depending on their race. For purposes of simplicity, you decide to measure *race* in terms of only two categories (white, non-white). *Personal income* is measured by the net personal income line on the previous year's tax return.

Independent variable: _____

Justification: _____

_____

_____

Categorical or numeric: _____

Justification: _____

_____

_____

Dependent variable: _____

Justification: _____

_____

_____

Categorical or numeric: _____

Justification: _____

_____

_____

Hypothesis: _____

_____

_____

Deriving deductive hypotheses

Suppose you have data that allow you to investigate deviance among individuals in different Canadian provinces. You look for sociological theories to guide your investigation, and you want to develop hypotheses derived from these theoretical ideas.

Your search of the literature leads you to select three well-known sociological theories to guide your investigation—control theory, conflict theory, and labelling theory.[1] We sketch each of these theories below, as well as some variables associated with them.

Using the variables provided, create a good-quality hypothesis for each of the three theories. On the basis of the theory in question, justify why you expect the particular relationship specified in each of your hypotheses.

Control theory

Brym et al.[2] argue:

> According to control theory, the rewards of deviance and crime are many. Proponents of this approach argue that nearly everyone wants fun, pleasure, excitement, and profit. Moreover, they say, if we could get away with it, most of us would commit deviant and criminal acts to acquire more of these valued things. For control theorists, the reason most of us don't engage in deviance and crime is that we are prevented from doing so. The

reason deviants and criminals break norms and laws is that social controls are insufficient to ensure their conformity.

Suppose that you have access to official statistics on crimes committed in Canada in 2008. Specify and justify a hypothesis that you could use to compare provinces and test control theory as an explanation for deviance, using the following two variables:

- *Maximum penalty for an impaired driving conviction*: The maximum penalty (months of jail time) allowable under provincial law for driving while under the influence of drugs or alcohol, regardless of whether or not an accident or injury occurred. For the sake of simplicity, let's exclude fines, conditional sentences, and other penalties from our variable and pretend that all sentences are measured in months of jail time (e.g., a maximum penalty of 12 months in jail, 20 months in jail, and so on).
- *Young impaired driver accident rate*: The number of accidents involving an impaired driver under the age of 20 per 1,000 drivers under age 20 in a province (e.g., 15 accidents per 1,000 drivers).

Hypothesis: _____

_____

Theory-based justification: _____

_____

_____

_____

Conflict theory
According to Brym et al.[3]:

> In brief, conflict theorists maintain that the rich and the powerful impose deviant and criminal labels on the less powerful members of society, particularly those who challenge the existing social order. Meanwhile, they are usually able to use their money and influence to escape punishment for their own misdeeds. . . . Steven Spitzer (1980) conveniently summarizes this school of thought. He notes that capitalist societies are based on private ownership of property. Moreover, their smooth functioning depends on the availability of productive labour and respect for authority. When thieves steal, they challenge private property. Theft is therefore a crime. . . . Of course, Spitzer adds, the rich and the powerful engage in deviant and criminal acts too. But, he adds, they tend to be dealt with more leniently. Industries can grievously harm people by damaging the environment, yet serious charges are rarely brought against the owners of industry. . . . Laws and norms may change along with shifts in the distribution of power in society. However, according to conflict

theorists, definitions of deviance and crime, and also punishments for misdeeds, are always influenced by who's on top.

Suppose that you have access to data recorded by the criminal justice system. Specify and justify a hypothesis that you could use to compare sentences and test conflict theory as an explanation for deviance, using the following two variables:

- *Severity of sentence*: Length of sentence (number of years of incarceration given to an individual for a criminal conviction). For the sake of simplicity, let's exclude fines, conditional sentences, and other penalties from this variable and pretend that all sentences are given in terms of years of incarceration.
- *Type of crime*: Type of crime for which the sentenced offender has been convicted, under two categories: street crime (e.g., prostitution, drug dealing) and white-collar crime (e.g., embezzlement, tax fraud).

Hypothesis: _____

_____

Theory-based justification: _____

_____

_____

_____

Labelling theory
According to Brym et al.[4]:

> A chief insight of labelling theory is that deviance results not just from the actions of the deviant but also from the responses of others, who define some actions as deviant and other actions as normal. . . . For example, if an adolescent misbehaves in school a few times, teachers and the principal may punish him. However, his troubles really begin if the school authorities and the police label him as a delinquent or, more formally, as a young offender. Surveillance of his actions will increase. Actions that authorities would normally not notice or would define as of little consequence are more likely to be interpreted as proof that he, indeed, is a delinquent or criminal 'type'. He may be ostracized from nondeviant cliques in the school and eventually socialized into a deviant subculture. Over time, immersion in the deviant subculture may lead the adolescent to adopt 'delinquent' as his master status, or overriding public identity. More easily than we may care to believe, what starts out as a few incidents of misbehaviour can amplify into a criminal career because of labelling. . . . Thus, the labelling process [can act] as a self-fulfilling prophecy.

Suppose that you have access to data recorded by the criminal justice system following up on cases of individuals who had been arrested and placed on trial at least once during their teen years to see how their lives had unfolded by age 25. Specify and justify a hypothesis that you could use to compare individuals and test labelling theory as an explanation for deviance, using the following two variables:

- *Imprisonment after age 18*: Whether or not the individual had been incarcerated at least once after age 18 (categorized as incarcerated or not incarcerated).
- *Youth criminal conviction*: Whether or not the individual was found guilty in a court of law between the ages of 14 and 17 (categorized as convicted at least once or never convicted).

Hypothesis: _____

_____

Theory-based justification: _____

_____

_____

_____

Note: Remember to consult the 'Tips for lab applications' section on the companions website (www.oupcanada.com/methodscoach) if you find you need help.

LAB 2
Errors in Reasoning

▶ Tune-up

The 'science game', as it is sometimes called, essentially involves two components—gathering evidence and thinking. The 'gathering evidence' component is associated with the 'methodological' aspects of science, while the 'thinking' (reasoning) component is associated with the 'theoretical' aspects. Of course, there is considerable overlap and interaction between these components. This lab highlights several errors in reasoning associated with scientific practice.

The following topics supplement your course readings and are intended to review some of the principal points you will need to understand in order to complete the lab questions related to common 'thinking errors'.

The context of relationships

The sign that a relationship exists is evident when there is a *systematic change* between the independent and dependent variables. Paralleling your experience in everyday life, independent and dependent variables are 'strangers' when both change but do so unsystematically. Conversely, the more systematic the change between the objects (either variables or people), the stronger the connection between them.

Relationships between people do not exist in isolation, and the same is true of relationships between independent and dependent variables. Instead, connections between variables and people always exist in some context.

In research, the 'context' of a relationship is specified by another kind of variable called a 'control' variable. Control variables are also called 'third' or 'conditional' variables. In practice, of course, the context of a relationship can include many variables, so it is possible to identify several control or third (i.e., fourth, fifth, and so on) variables for any particular independent–dependent variable relationship. So, for example, although two sweethearts may declare their undying love (relationship) for one another on Saturday night, they probably know this declaration is conditional: 'But what will they say when they're sober?' In a parallel way, the relationship between family income and higher education in various countries may 'depend' (i.e., be conditional) on whether the national post-secondary system is tuition-based or state-funded.

Genuine and phoney relationships

Another way of saying that a relationship exists between independent and dependent variables is to say that the variables are 'correlated'. Correlation simply means the variables are associated or change together. But as in life, the appearance of a relationship between two variables does not always signify that the relationship is 'real'. Appearances and reality do not always coincide—just ask any sweetheart with a broken heart.

One reason for the imperfect alignment between the appearance and reality of relationships is the operation of third/control variables. The operation of these conditional variables can affect the nature of an apparent independent–dependent variable relationship. One goal of the scientific enterprise is to distinguish 'real' relationships from 'apparent' ones. Consequently, before a researcher is prepared to declare that a relationship between two variables is 'genuine' or 'authentic', the potential influence of possibly contaminating third variables is typically investigated. Researchers perform this exercise to avoid being fooled—that is, to avoid the thinking error of believing that 'what is apparent is real'.

The idea of spuriousness

When a relationship is evident between independent and dependent variables, it may be genuine (i.e., an authentic connection), or it may be phoney. Researchers label phoney or inauthentic relationships 'spurious'. To understand why an inauthentic relationship between two variables may appear real, you need to recall that *variables have their effects when they change (vary)*. This is true of all variables, *including the third variables that form the 'context' for an independent–dependent variable relationship.*

Spuriousness occurs when the change (variation) in a contextual variable causes changes in both the independent and dependent variables. Figure 2.1 illustrates this circumstance.

Figure 2.1 Spurious relationships

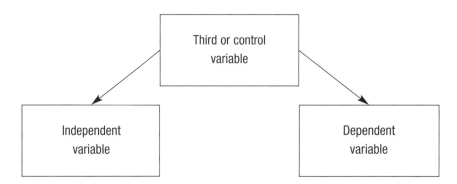

Notice that the independent and dependent variables are not 'really' connected (i.e., there is no line connecting them). Follow the arrows to see how the spurious situation operates. Variation in the third variable *causes changes in both the independent and dependent variables*. Consequently, if you *only looked at the independent and dependent variables* (i.e., if you did not note the context), you would *see the independent and dependent variables changing together systematically*. Under spurious circumstances, you would see that the independent and dependent variables are related when in fact they are not. In short, you would be fooled by phoney appearances.

Testing for spuriousness

Nobody likes to be fooled unwittingly, including researchers. To protect themselves against such embarrassment, researchers have a way of testing for potential spuriousness in an independent–dependent variable relationship. The easiest way to understand the test for spuriousness is to contrast the 'spuriousness' diagram (Figure 2.1) with the following diagram of what a 'genuine' relationship looks like (Figure 2.2).

Figure 2.2 Genuine relationships

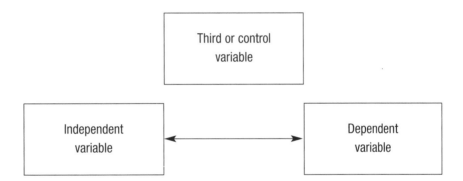

In the 'genuine' diagram, the independent and dependent variables are *actually related*, as evidenced by the double-headed arrow connecting them. Moreover, the third variable is *not connected* to either the independent or the dependent variable.

Comparing the spurious and genuine diagrams, we see that the operation of the third variable has either *nothing to do* with the independent–dependent variable connection (the 'genuine' case) or *everything to do* with the appearance of such a connection (the 'spurious' case).

Based on this crucial difference between authentic and inauthentic relationships, researchers have devised a test for determining the existence of spuriousness. The key idea of the test is to examine the independent–dependent variable relationship under two conditions—first, when the third variable is allowed to *change (vary)* and second, when the third variable is *held constant*. (By the way, it is under this second condition that third variables are sometimes termed 'control' variables, since their effects are held in check.)

Using these comparisons, here is how the test for spuriousness works. If the independent–dependent variable relationship is *authentic*, then a *relationship will be evident under both conditions* (i.e., when the third variable is allowed to vary and when it is held constant). By contrast, if the original relationship is *spurious*, an independent–dependent variable connection will be *evident* when the third variable is *changing* (the first condition) and *disappear* when the third variable is held *constant* (the second condition).

This understanding parallels situations in everyday life. Those with whom we have an authentic connection stick with us no matter what the outside conditions (sickness or health, richness or poorness, and so on). When relationships are inauthentic, they disappear when the influence of external circumstances is removed.

What is observed

A variable is used to detect diversity in some property of an object. Detecting diversity requires researchers to measure the objects under consideration. In research, each 'object' that is measured constitutes a 'case'. A case is the smallest unit from which a researcher collects data.

In sociology and other social sciences, cases can be of different sizes. In other words, the 'units' being studied can be of varying sizes. Such differences in the sizes of the objects of research are identified by the term 'units of analysis'.

When researchers refer to 'units of analysis', they are inquiring about whether the objects of investigation are persons, groups, cities, political parties, nations, and so on. Researchers are free to choose whatever unit of analysis is most appropriate for the research issue under consideration. The important point is that researchers are clear on what the unit of analysis is in any particular study.

Ecological fallacy

All fallacies are 'thinking errors'; they result when we make mistakes in reasoning. One such error in reasoning related to units of analysis is called the 'ecological fallacy'.

As noted, not all research studies use the same unit of analysis. Although it is common for 'individuals' to comprise the cases in a study, units larger than persons (e.g., provinces, states) are often the objects of study. The data related to these larger units of analysis are usually 'aggregated' from individual data. For example, 'provincial crime rate' is such an aggregation.

In most cases, aggregated data inform us about social and institutional contexts surrounding the individual. People live in communities with varying levels of integration, in provinces with differing unemployment rates, and in nations with diverse levels of literacy. Because units of analysis that are 'aggregated' tell us about social surroundings, they are also called 'ecological data'.

It is important to keep in mind the following fundamental point of interpretation related to units of analysis: *the evidence collected only tells us about the unit of analysis of the cases under consideration*. In other words, when data are collected from individuals, they inform us about individuals; when the cases are provinces, we can only make conclusions about provinces.

When we fail to limit our inferences to the units of analysis under consideration, we risk making errors in reasoning (fallacies). One such error is the 'ecological fallacy'.

The ecological fallacy (also called the 'wrong-level fallacy') occurs when inferences about *individual* units of analysis are made from data gathered at some *aggregate (ecological)* unit of analysis. In other words, the risk of the ecological fallacy occurs when information about aggregates (e.g., communities, provinces, nations) is used to draw conclusions about the individuals who comprise these aggregates.

Consider the following simple illustration: The average income in two neighbourhoods is calculated and found to be $50,000. Note that the unit of analysis here is 'neighbourhood' and the finding is an 'aggregate' measure. Are you confident in concluding that *most individuals* in these neighbourhoods have incomes of $50,000? If you were to draw such a conclusion, it would be at the risk of committing the ecological fallacy. The 'average income' tells us about the neighbourhood; it does not tell us about the individuals. For example, while one of the communities may be comprised only of $50,000 earners, the other could be comprised only of people earning either much more or much less than $50,000. Yet both communities could have average incomes of $50,000.

Creating mental maps

Researchers are interested in helping us better understand some phenomenon of interest. Common tests of what it means to 'understand' something include the ability to either explain or predict it. For example, your understanding of why a community is relatively poor will expand if a sociologist 'explains' the causes of the community's poverty. Similarly, the ability of an astronomer to predict precisely when and where the next total eclipse of the sun will occur is convincing evidence that she 'understands' the phenomenon.

In other words, researchers expand our understanding of a topic by providing us with a mental map. The mental map shows how the object of interest is related to other things. These other things may include 'causes' and 'effects'. Whatever the case, the mental maps provided through research tell us about 'relationships' between things.

Identification versus explanation

The first step in understanding something is being able to identify it. Something is identified when we can 'name' it. Such 'naming' is done by 'labelling' the object of interest with a 'concept'. This process is one way in which reality is constructed, following the adage 'First we "look", then we "name", and finally we "see".' In this way, your reality becomes enlarged when you learn to appropriately label diffuse experience with concepts such as 'shame', 'role strain', 'Oedipal complex', or 'cultural lag'.

Although identification is necessary for understanding, it is not sufficient. In other words, just because we can recognize and label some experience does not mean that we understand it. Recognizing that your sweetheart is a 'neurotic' rather than a 'psychotic' is a helpful first step, but it should not be confused with a full understanding of his or her conduct.

Explanation requires moving beyond identification to *relating* the object identified to other associated things. For example, you improve your understanding when you see how current levels of shame are related to early childhood experiences, how complexity of role sets leads to enhanced role strain, or how unresolved Oedipal complexes generate adult fixations on pornography. The key to explanation is to appreciate that it relates something *to something else*.

Tautologies

Tautologies are thinking errors that occur when our reasoning is 'circular'. As noted, enhanced understanding occurs when we relate an object of interest to something else and, in doing so, expand our mental map. When formulated in terms of a statement, the object of interest is in the 'subject' of the sentence, while what it is related to is in the 'predicate' of the sentence. The statement 'People with higher levels of education generally enjoy high earned incomes' improves our understanding of the 'subject' (education) by expressing its relationship to something else (income) in the predicate.

Tautologies (the error of 'circular reasoning') occur when a statement 'predicates nothing'. In other words, tautologies occur when the subject is repeated in the predicate of a statement. Here are some rather amusing examples:

- A politician's explanation for losing an election: 'I simply didn't get enough votes.'
- Gertrude Stein's famous proclamation at Harvard University: 'A rose is a rose is a rose.'
- Yogi Berra's mother's observation about his premature baldness: 'You know, Yogi, you wouldn't be so bald if you had more hair.'

And you may find the following comment by former prime minister Jean Chrétien amusing—or perhaps chilling:

> When he [Chrétien] was tackled about the absence of proof that his government's Quebec sponsorship program [later proved to have been criminally fraudulent] made sense, he replied: 'The proof is the proof. And when you have a good proof, it's proven.'[1]

The problem with tautologies is that they fool us into a false appreciation of our level of understanding. Rather than expanding our understanding and enlarging our mental map by connecting different things, they leave us mentally 'spinning our wheels'. We learn nothing from tautologies because they lead us around in a circle.

Not all tautologies are easily identified. It is clear to all of us that we learn nothing about a rose from Ms Stein, nothing about Yogi's baldness from his mother, and nothing from the politician's insight that election losses are defined by vote shortages. However, tautologies can *appear* more sophisticated when they use *different words* to talk about the subject in the predicate. No matter what its appearance, any statement that does not advance our thinking (i.e., that leads us nowhere) cannot help to improve our understanding.

LAB 2 APPLICATION

Learning objectives

The following lab questions are directed at helping you translate the tune-up points into concrete research situations. Specifically, this lab assignment challenges you to clarify your understanding of:

- the operation of spurious reasoning;
- inferences based on the ecological fallacy;
- the existence of tautological thinking.

Assessing spuriousness

If you follow news reports for an extended period, the following pattern will become evident: the greater the number of firefighters present at the site of a fire, the greater the evident fire damage (measured in dollars). Based on this observation, the following conclusion seems apparent: *the more firefighters appearing at the site of a fire, the greater the extent of fire damage.*

This conclusion could be stated in research terms as follows: There is a positive relationship between the number of firefighters appearing at the site of a fire and the extent of fire damage. This is a potentially frightening relationship, which might deter you from calling the fire department if you see a building in flames. After all, you want to limit the amount of fire damage, and it appears that one way of doing so is to limit the number of firefighters on the scene.

However, the reasoning leading to such a conclusion is flawed. To understand why this is so, complete the diagram below by:

a. identifying the *independent* variable and placing it in the appropriate box;
b. identifying the *dependent* variable and placing it in the appropriate box;
c. thinking of a key *control* variable for this situation and placing it in the appropriate box;
d. providing an explanation of the *reasoning* you would employ to conclude that the independent–dependent variable relationship is *spurious.*

Figure 2.3

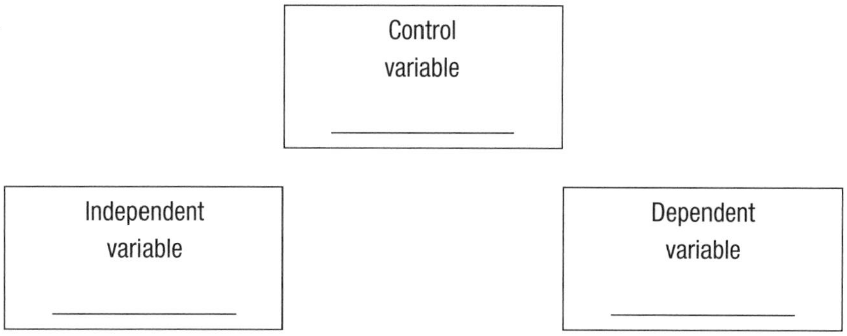

```
                    ┌─────────────────┐
                    │     Control     │
                    │     variable    │
                    │                 │
                    │   _____   │
                    └─────────────────┘


┌─────────────────┐                    ┌─────────────────┐
│   Independent   │                    │    Dependent    │
│     variable    │                    │     variable    │
│                 │                    │                 │
│   _____   │                    │   _____   │
└─────────────────┘                    └─────────────────┘
```

Explanation: _____

_____

_____

_____

_____

_____

_____

_____

_____

Here is another example to sharpen your reasoning. *In Europe, the evidence consistently shows that the number of storks in a region is related to the number of babies born in the region.*

Identify and justify the independent and dependent variables in this proposition.

_____

_____

State the research hypothesis implied by the proposition.

_____

_____

Identify and justify a third variable that might contribute to the hypothesis being spurious.

_____

_____

Complete the diagram below, and explain what tests could be conducted that would lead to a conclusion of spuriousness.

Figure 2.4

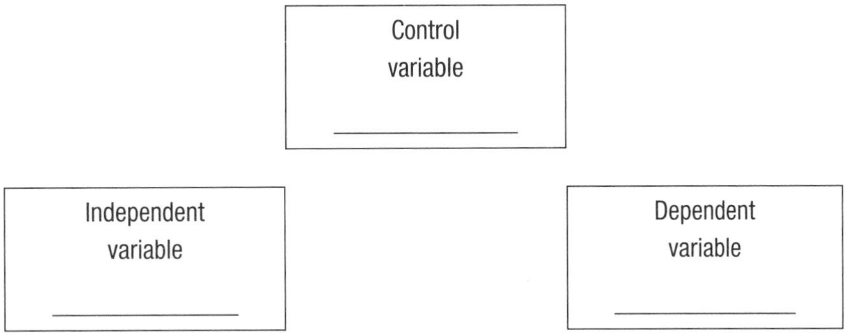

Reasoning:

In this particular example, what does it mean to say that the 'third variable is allowed to vary'?

_____

_____

In this particular example, what does it mean to say that the 'third variable is held constant'?

_____

_____

If the relationship is *authentic*, what would you expect to see under the two conditions above?

_____

_____

If the relationship is *spurious*, what would you expect to see under the two conditions above?

_____

_____

Which of the authentic versus spurious considerations seems more plausible and why?

_____

_____

Units of analysis

Every year, the Ig® Nobel Prizes are awarded at Harvard University to 'celebrate the unusual, honor the imaginative—and spur people's interest in science, medicine, and technology'. The 2004 Ig® Nobel Prize for Medicine was awarded to sociologists Steven Stack and Jim Gundlach for a study in which they compared country music airtime and suicide rates for 49 large American metropolitan areas. Their central finding, as noted in the abstract of their article, was as follows:

The greater the radio airtime devoted to country music, the greater the white suicide rate.

The variable 'radio airtime devoted to country music' was measured in terms of the percentage of airtime devoted to country music, while the variable 'suicide rate'[2] was measured as the number of suicides per 100,000 of the white population. The findings showed that cities with a higher percentage of country music played had higher suicide rates than cities with a lower percentage of country music played.

The authors reasoned that 'Country music is hypothesized to nurture a suicidal mood through its concerns with problems common in the suicidal population, such as marital discord, alcohol abuse, and alienation from work.'[3] They used various control variables, such as SES (socio-economic status) in order to test for spuriousness.

What is the independent variable in this study? _____

What is the dependent variable? _____

Identify and justify the unit of analysis of the independent and dependent variables:

Unit of analysis: _____

Justification: _____

_____

_____

A newspaper report on the sociologists' article concluded that their study demonstrated that 'listening to country music encourages listeners to commit suicide.'

Explain how this conclusion is at risk of employing the ecological fallacy:

_____

_____

_____

_____

_____

Below are plausible findings from the research literature. For each finding, write a conclusion that could be drawn *at the risk of committing the ecological fallacy*.

Based on data from neighbourhoods across a city, it is evident that there is a strong association between unemployment rates and rates of crime.

_____

_____

_____

Nations that contain a higher proportion of Protestants generally have higher suicide rates.

_____

_____

_____

Communities with higher average incomes have lower rates of mental illness.

_____

_____

_____

Regions with a higher percentage of elderly people have higher crime rates.

_____

_____

_____

Tautological reasoning

The following list of statements is comprised of tautologies. Point out the circular reasoning evident in each case.

You can observe an awful lot just by watching.

_____

_____

Jeffrey is in prison because he was convicted of murder.

_____

_____

The felon robbed the bank because that's where the money was.

_____

_____

Below are excerpts from two clinical cases related to expert testimony provided by psychiatrists.[4] For each case, explain how tautological reasoning is in operation.

Case 1

Probation: Why, doctor, does our client continue to steal?

Psychiatry: He is suffering from antisocial reaction.

Probation: What are the marks of 'antisocial reaction'?

Psychiatry: Persistent thievery is one symptom.

Tautological reasoning:

_____

_____

_____

_____

Case 2

Defence: Whether one calls him insane or psychotic, he's a sick man. That's obvious.

Psychiatry: I should think that's largely a matter of terminology.

Defence: Do you mean to suggest that a man could do what that boy has done [murdered and butchered a young woman] and not be sick?

Tautological reasoning:

_____

_____

_____

_____

The following examples from the sociological literature contain tautologies that are more 'sophisticated' in the sense that they are less evident.[5] For each example, identify and explain the tautology in operation.

Example 1

In a famous *American Journal of Sociology* article, 'On becoming a marijuana user', Howard Becker (1953: 241) provides the following reasoning to account for why some people use the drug:

A person, then, cannot begin to use marijuana for pleasure, or continue its use for pleasure, unless he learns to define its effects as enjoyable, unless it becomes and remains an object which he conceives as capable of producing pleasure.

Operation of tautological reasoning:

_____

_____

_____

_____

_____

Example 2

The famous social anthropologist Clyde Kluckhohn, in his 1949 book *Mirror for Man*, defines 'culture' as a people's 'way of life'. In one of his illustrations, he notes that the Chinese do not like milk. In accounting for this aversion to milk, Kluckhohn explains that the Chinese do not like milk 'because of their culture'.

Operation of tautological reasoning:

_____

_____

_____

_____

_____

Note: Remember to consult the 'Tips for lab applications' section on the companion website (www.oupcanada.com/methodscoach) if you find you need help.

LAB 3
Conceptual and Operational Definitions

▶ Tune-up

Experience without understanding

Sociologists continually remind us that a key determinant of our experience is what we have learned through socialization. This theme is so strong in the literature that the term 'humanization' is used as a synonym for socialization. We become 'human' through what we learn from others. The implication is that newborn infants, although teeming with potential, are not fully developed in their humanity.

If our experience is heavily determined by our socialization, and if newborns are only beginning their socialization journey, it is interesting to ask what their experience of life might be like. Given that the newborn's sensors (i.e., sight, sound, taste, smell, touch) are healthy and operating, the famous psychologist/philosopher William James described its initial encounters with the world outside the womb as a 'booming, buzzing confusion'. In short, the newborn's experience must be 'wild'.

If others have done an adequate job, and your socialization is relatively complete, we can safely assume that your experience of the world is far less frightening than that of a newborn infant, less 'raw', because you have been taught to *understand* what is occurring to and around you.

Concepts as organizing terms

A key to the refinement of your experience and understanding centres on the use of concepts. Concepts are abstract categories used for organizing our sensory experience. The key to understanding the notion of concepts is the term 'abstract'.

The abstract level of experience is typically contrasted against the concrete level. Where concrete experience is composed of empirical sensations, abstract experience involves mental images. In contrast to concrete experience, which resides in your sensors, abstract experience resides in your mind.

The root of the term 'abstract' literally means 'to drop away'. A simple example demonstrates the operation of this dropping away: Select any five pens, and place them on a desk or table. If you examine these five objects in terms of their 'concreteness', you will observe that they are distinctly different. They may be different sizes, colours, shapes; some may be new, while others may have teeth marks or other signs of use. Note, however, that you apply the same label to all these different objects—the concept 'pen'.

You are so expert at such conceptualization that you may see nothing remarkable in such a seemingly trivial act, but you would be wrong. What you have actually done is perform a sophisticated mental feat. To correctly label these very different objects as 'pens', you had to mentally 'drop away' (i.e., disregard) most of their attributes and focus on only two of their many characteristics—namely, that they are all writing objects and that they use ink. In this way, the multiple dimensions of 'sense experience' have been 'organized' through the application of a concept.

By organizing our raw/wild sense experience, concepts help us to understand what is occurring within, around, and to us. By providing us with such understanding, concepts serve as a primary vehicle through which our experience becomes meaningful. This process is a matter of continuing education; the meaning in our lives becomes larger as the number and diversity of the concepts we command grow. For example, the mark of a liberally educated person is that she has 'come to terms' with a broader, more diverse range of concepts than an ignorant individual has.

Concepts and communication

Concepts are used to identify and label our experience. When we are able to recognize the Big Dipper in the night sky, or racism in a society, or role conflict in ourselves, our experience becomes more meaningful than it would otherwise be. But we also employ these same concepts to share our experience with others. We use concepts to communicate with others—to tell them, for example, that the Big Dipper is very clear tonight, that racism is pervasive in our city, or that we feel drained because of role conflict.

Recall, however, that each of us learned the meaning of most concepts from others through acts of socialization. For example, your father may have taught you what a gooseberry is, your grandmother what guilt is like, and your sociology professor the meaning of institutional racism. And here lie the seeds of trouble. Most of us do not share the same fathers, grandmothers, or sociology professors—and this causes real problems, since my father may never have told me what a gooseberry is, my grandmother might have a different notion of guilt, and my sociology professor might have given a poor lecture on institutional racism.

In short, when we use concepts to communicate, we rely on a very important and tenuous assumption—namely, that both the sender and the receiver of the message have been *socialized* to give the *same meaning* to the *same concept*. Given that we all have different teachers, what is the realistic chance of this happening? Ask anyone whose heart has been broken because of a mistaken assumption that sender and receiver attribute the same meaning to the potent little phrase 'I love you.'

Defining our terms

Since the meaning of concepts is rooted in our socialization, and our respective socializations are quite distinct, it is little wonder that there is so much miscommunication. It is even plausible that the reverse is worthy of admiration: Given the risks inherent in our differing socializations, it is incredible that there is as much clear communication as there is!

In everyday life, of course, we do not always assume that communications are clear. We often question and request clarification: 'What did you mean by that?' 'I am not sure I understand what you are saying, so can you please elaborate.' In research, where it is particularly important that communications are clear, we usually provide clarification even before it is requested. Such conceptual clarification is given through definitions. In particular, researchers commonly rely on two types of definitions—conceptual and operational.

Conceptual definitions

Recall that concepts are abstract (imaginary) terms. When we claim to understand the meaning of a term, we mean that we share a 'common' mental image of the term's referents. For instance, it is quite likely that we share similar mental images of concepts such as Big Mac, banana split, and compact disk. By contrast, it is likely that shared mental images are fuzzier for such concepts as intelligence or mechanical solidarity.

One way we can help to ensure that we share the same mental images associated with a concept is to provide a conceptual definition. A conceptual definition helps to clarify the meaning of a concept by *expressing it in other concepts*. In this way, conceptual definitions operate at the abstract level of experience. Abstract concepts are defined in terms of other abstract concepts. Conceptual definitions are the kind found in most dictionaries, where a concept whose meaning you do not know is expressed in terms of concepts you do know. Dictionaries using conceptual definitions tell us what a term means 'in other words'. 'Intelligence', for example, is the 'ability to think abstractly'; 'mechanical solidarity' is 'a form of integration based on similarity between individuals'.

Conceptual definitions are intended to help us clarify our understanding of a concept. Some conceptual definitions are better than others in helping us achieve this goal. Better-quality conceptual definitions are distinguished from poorer-quality ones in their effective employment of three criteria.

The first requirement of good conceptual definitions is *clarity*. Recall that we typically require conceptual definitions for terms whose meaning we do not understand. Therefore, it is important that the definition of the term *uses words whose meaning we do (or are likely to) understand*. In this sense, clarity comes from simplicity. We prefer that a conceptual definition uses terms that are as simple as possible to assist our understanding.

The second criterion for assessing conceptual definitions is *concreteness*. We consult conceptual definitions to obtain a description of what the communicator had in mind when he or she used the term. Toward this end, it is helpful if the definitions are as concrete as possible. Evaluative (judgmental) language is not helpful on this account.

Finally, conceptual definitions should be as *complete* as possible. Many things that we wish to distinguish between are very similar to one another (e.g., chickadees and junkos). Such similarity raises a risk of confusion (e.g., role conflict as opposed to role strain). An important task of conceptual definitions is to provide enough information (i.e., be sufficiently complete) that consumers are alerted to the relevant distinctions between closely related phenomena.

Operational definitions

Conceptual definitions function at the abstract level and are successful to varying degrees at clarifying our understanding. Operational definitions offer an alternate approach to such clarification.

Operational definitions provide an understanding of a concept *by linking the abstract to the concrete level of experience.* In this form, an abstract concept is defined by identifying the steps followed to experience its meaning in a concrete manner. In other words, operational definitions provide the procedures (i.e., the 'operations') required to observe a concept. While a conceptual definition of 'intelligence' might state that it is 'the ability to think abstractly', an operational definition would tell us how to 'see' intelligence through the administration and scoring of a standardized IQ test. Similarly, the conceptual definition of 'mechanical solidarity' as 'a form of integration based on similarity between individuals' might be 'operationalized' through societal-level observations such as structural tightness, the prevalence of repressive law, and a high level of collectivity orientation.

Operational definitions specify the rules to follow in order to experience a concept. In this sense, they are much like a recipe. (The dictionary definition of a lemon soufflé may evoke a vision of this delicious dessert, but the vision is a far cry from the mouth-watering result of a good recipe.) Just as some recipes are better guides than others, operational definitions vary in their utility. Operational definitions are evaluated in terms of two principal criteria.

The first criterion for evaluating operational definitions relates to conceptual definitions. Conceptual definitions provide us with an abstract vision of what we have in mind, while operational definitions concretize that vision. Therefore, we want operational definitions to *capture all the relevant dimensions* identified in a term's conceptual definition. Without this connection to conceptual understanding, operational definitions risk creating an Alice in Wonderland world.[1]

The second criterion for assessing operational definitions is *step specification*. The goal of operational definitions is to provide a systematic link to the concrete level of experience so that we can *experience* what the concept under consideration means. This connection requires that the steps (i.e., the operations) to be performed be sufficiently clear and complete that other people can establish the same linkage to the sensory world.

Lab 3 Application

Learning objectives

The following lab questions are directed at helping you translate the tune-up points into concrete research situations. Specifically, this lab assignment challenges you to clarify your understanding of:

- how conceptual definitions are constructed;
- how operational definitions are created;
- how ideologies affect preferred definitions.

Operationalizing health

Throughout the world, people are concerned about their health; some are even obsessed with it. But what does it mean to be 'healthy'? The World Health Organization provides the following *conceptual definition*:

A state of complete physical, mental and social well-being and not merely the absence of disease or infirmity.[2]

On the basis of this conceptual definition, provide an *operational definition* for assessing a person's health.

_____

_____

_____

Conceptualizing poverty

Poverty is an important issue in most societies. But what does it mean to be poor? To begin thinking about this concept, identify whether each of the following components is part of your understanding of 'poverty'. In the space provided, justify your consideration.

Homeless?[3]

_____

_____

_____

Jobless?

_____

_____

_____

Starving?

_____

_____

_____

Living in the Third World?

_____

_____

_____

Given your reflections, provide a *conceptual definition* of what it means to be 'poor':

_____

_____

_____

_____

Implications of alternative definitions: Poverty in Canada

Contrary to popular belief, the Government of Canada has no official definition of poverty, nor does it set an official poverty line. However, Statistics Canada has designed three measures that allow researchers and policy-makers to assess the prevalence of low income in Canada, although in practice many researchers treat these measures as indicators of poverty. These three measures include the Low Income Cut-off (LICO), the Low Income Measure (LIM), and the Market Basket Measure (MBM).

The LICO and LIM measures reflect a definition that poverty means a household having low income relative to other households of the same size. By contrast, the MBM reflects a definition of poverty centred on a household not having enough income to buy a specific basket of goods and services in the local community. Not surprisingly, these three measures each produce a *different picture* of the prevalence of poverty in Canada.

Below are definitions of each of the three measures of low income as well as illustrations of the application of each measure. Review the definitions, and work through the illustrations until you feel comfortable with the meaning of each approach.

1. Low Income Cut-off (LICO)
   - Defined as the income below which a family is likely to spend 20 percentage points *more* of its income on food, shelter, and clothing than the *average family*.
   - For example, if the percentage of total income (before taxes) spent on food, clothing, and shelter by the average Canadian household is 34.7 per cent, a family is considered to be in 'straitened circumstances' (i.e., experiencing financial strain) if it spends 54.7 per cent (i.e., 34.7 + 20) of its income on these items. Statistics Canada then calculates the income at which it estimates that a family will reach that 54.7 per cent.

2. Low Income Measure (LIM)
   - Defined as 'half the median family income (income is adjusted for family size)'.[4]
   - For example, if the median family income for a family of two adults and two children in Canada is $20,000, the LIM would be $10,000.

3. Market Basket Measure (MBM)
   - Looks at typical local expenditures in five categories (i.e., a 'basket') for a family of two adults and two children: food, clothing, shelter, transportation, other household needs (e.g., telephone service). 'Any household with a level of income lower than the cost of the basket is considered to be living on low income.'[5]
   - Unlike LICO and LIM, MBM considers differences in the cost of living among specific communities (e.g., Toronto versus Winnipeg) as well as the availability of 'disposable income' after expenditures on such things as child care (not just on food, clothing, and shelter) are deducted.

Using these three different definitions, the percentage of Canadian children 'living in poverty' has been estimated as:

Low Income Cut-off (LICO) method:	12.6%
Low Income Measure (LIM) method:	13.5%
Market Basket Measure (MBM) method:	16.9%

The differences in these estimates are dramatic. For example, using MBM results in a *34 per cent larger estimate* of children living in 'poverty' than the LICO method. It is not surprising, therefore, that different orientations will find some definitions of 'poverty' more congenial than others.

Political ideology is one type of orientation that conditions viewpoints on various issues, including poverty. One simple classification of political orientation is the 'liberal–conservative' distinction:

Liberal or left-wing voters promote extensive government involvement in the economy. Among other things, this means they favor a strong 'social safety net' of health and welfare benefits to help the less fortunate members of society. As a result, liberal policies often lead to less economic inequality. In contrast, *conservative or right-wing* voters favor a reduced role for government in the economy. They favor a smaller welfare state and emphasize the importance of individual initiative in promoting economic growth.[6]

Liberals tend to advocate that *change* is needed, while conservatives tend to support the *status quo*.

Suppose that you are a policy analyst interested in preparing research to support a liberal or left-wing political party's election campaign with relevant statistics. You have the choice of using the LICO, the LIM, or the MBM. Thinking specifically about the differences in the prevalence of children living in poverty between the three measures, which measure should you choose? Justify your choice.

Liberal choice: _____

Justification: _____

_____

_____

Suppose that you switch allegiances and are now a policy analyst interested in preparing research to support a conservative or right-wing political party's election campaign with relevant statistics. Which would be your preferred child poverty measure and why?

Conservative choice: _____

Justification: _____

_____

_____

Operationalizing powerlessness

Melvin Seeman is famous for his research on the topic of alienation. In Seeman's view, alienation has several dimensions, one of which is powerlessness. Early in his career, Seeman and his colleague Arthur Neal[7] published a classic article in which he defined and operationalized powerlessness.

Conceptually, Neal and Seeman defined powerlessness as a low expectation of control over events, as lack of control over the political system, the industrial economy, and international affairs. Their basic idea was that the experience of powerlessness revolves around subjectively held probabilities that the outcome of political and economic events cannot be controlled by oneself or, collectively, by persons like oneself.

To operationalize their idea, they provided respondents with the following seven pairs of statements and asked them to select the statement from each pair that came closest to their opinion.

1. I think we have adequate means for preventing runaway inflation.
   There's very little we can do to keep prices from going higher.
2. Persons like myself have little chance of protecting our personal interests when they conflict with those of strong pressure groups.
   I feel that we have adequate ways of coping with pressure groups.
3. A lasting world peace can be achieved by those of us who work toward it.
   There's very little we can do to bring about permanent world peace.
4. There's very little persons like myself can do to improve world opinion of Canada.
   I think each of us can do a great deal to improve world opinion of Canada.
5. This world is run by a few people in power, and there is not much the little guy can do about it.
   The average citizen can have an influence on government decisions.
6. It is only wishful thinking to believe that one can really influence what happens to society at large.
   People like me can change the course of world events if we make ourselves heard.
7. More and more, I feel helpless in the face of what's happening in the world today.
   I sometimes feel personally to blame for the sad state of affairs in the world.

Using these pairs of statements, *identify a set of operations* that would lead to a measure of respondents' powerlessness on a scale ranging from 0 to 7.

Step 1

_____

_____

_____

Step 2

_____

_____

_____

Step 3

_____

_____

_____

Additional steps

_____

_____

_____

Note: Remember to consult the 'Tips for lab applications' section on the companion website (www.oupcanada.com/methodscoach) if you find you need help.

LAB 4
Levels of Measurement

▶ Tune-up

Variables as the tools of measurement

Variables are the working stuff of research. When a researcher can convert a problem or issue into one involving variables, an essential problem has been addressed.

Take an issue like the assumed connection between education and earnings. Is it really the case that better-educated people experience higher earnings than those with less education? To research this problem, the researcher faces the challenge of deciding what variable(s) to observe that will allow sorting people into different levels of education and which ones to observe in establishing levels of earnings. In short, 'education' and 'earnings' are concepts, and what the researcher requires are variables. Say, for example, 'number of years of schooling' is selected as the variable indicating education and 'net income reported on tax return' is chosen as the indicator of earnings. With these selections, the proposition relating education and earnings has now been translated into a researchable form about the relationship between variables.

Viewed in this way, the translation of concepts into variables is a first important step in the process of establishing operational definitions.

The meaning of measurement

While the translation of concepts into variables is an essential step in operationalization, it is not the only step. The goal of operational definitions is not simply to select or create variables for relevant concepts. The goal is to measure the amount of the variables' properties among a sample of objects of interest. We want to learn, for example, the 'number of years of schooling' and 'net income reported on tax return' a representative sample of Calgarians has. In short, operational definitions require measurement.

Measurement is a process. Specifically, it is the process of *systematically applying* a variable to an object. The key here is understanding what 'application' and 'systematic' mean in this context. You will recall that variables are composed of components called attributes. Attributes specify the mutually exclusive and exhaustive set of categories that comprise a variable. The attributes, in other words, identify all the possible 'scores' that a variable could take. Typically, the attributes of a variable are scored with numbers. For example, a person's gender might be scored with the alternatives 1 for male and 2 for female.

The application part of measurement now becomes evident. Application requires placing a number (representing the variable's score or attribute) on an object. A 2 is applied to Jane, a 1 to James. The application could be literal, but in most cases it is symbolic. Your instructor could, for example, give you your score on the first test by pasting a Post-it Note with your grade on your forehead (literal) but is more likely to record your score beside your name in the grade book (symbolic).

For proper measurement to occur, it is not sufficient to apply scores to objects; they must be applied systematically. In other words, the application of scores needs to follow some rules. The haphazard application of numbers cannot yield good-quality measures. You would justifiably object to an instructor assigning grades randomly. Instead, you expect grades to be assigned through an answer key, which serves as a template of rules for accumulating points on a test.

The goal of measurement

The goal of measurement is to *capture information*. More specifically, it is to capture information about a particular variable with respect to a particular object. For example, we want to learn how much after-tax income (the variable) Fredrika (the object) has.

In other words, measurement extracts (i.e., takes an imprint of) information about a variable from an object. The goal of a research methods test is to 'find out' what you know about the readings and lecture material. Once extracted, the information is in the researcher's possession.

It is important for a researcher to capture information about objects for two reasons. First, in most cases, the researcher is unable to 'keep' the objects of interest. A psychology professor is no better positioned to keep the subjects of her experiment after her investigation than an astronomer is to keep a comet after its properties have been measured. Second, even if researchers could keep the objects of their attention, there is a good chance that these objects will change. Students' aggression levels change, as does a comet's radiation level. In short, the objects will not be the same later on.

As a result, researchers take measures (i.e., readings) of objects and store them. Through the construction of variables that indicate concepts (i.e., operationalization) and the systematic application of variables to objects (i.e., measurement), researchers capture the information they require for later analysis.

Different types of differences

To repeat, the goal of measurement is to capture *information* about *differences* between objects in terms of a variable or variables. For example, respondents might express their attitude to the statement 'The prime minister of Canada is incompetent' on a 5-point scale including:

1. strongly agree
2. agree
3. neutral
4. disagree
5. strongly disagree

The difference between any two respondents' answers is identified by assigning each of them a number—one of them a 2 and the other a 5, for example. Long after the respondents have answered, these numbers allow the researcher to 'possess' information about their different attitudes on the subject under consideration.

A problem soon emerges, however, and this problem is related to the fact that the information captured by the measurement numbers *differs in terms of its complexity*. Take the following simple example. Imagine that you are asked to rate two folk songs on a 10-point scale ranging from 'a terrible folk song' (scored 1) to 'a magnificent folk song' (scored 10). Let's say you rate one of the folk songs as 3 and the other as 9. Clearly, these differences measure your rating of the quality of the different folk songs.

Now let's say you are asked to rate two symphonies on a 10-point scale ranging from 'a terrible symphony' (scored 1) to 'a magnificent symphony' (scored 10). And in this case, you rate one of the symphonies as 3 and the other as 9—again expressing your rating of the different qualities of the symphonies.

You can now easily compare the ratings (measures) of the two folk songs and identify the better one (scored 9). Likewise, you can compare the measurements of the symphonies and identify the one scoring 9 as the superior one. These are called *within class* differences because you are measuring differences within a particular 'class' of music (i.e., either folk song or symphony differences).

The following puzzling question now emerges: Is the 9 given to the folk song the same as (i.e., comparable to) the 9 given to the symphony? After all, they both look the same; they are both 9s. The answer is that these digits are *not* comparable even though they look identical. Even though they are both accurate measures, *they are not measuring the same thing*. One is a 'folk song 9', the other a 'symphonic 9'.

The differences between folk songs and symphonies are differences *between classes* of music. Folk songs are a relatively simple class of music (for example, you can play hundreds of folk songs if you know three simple chords), while symphonies constitute a more complex class of music. The folk song rating is a 'simple 9', while the symphony rating is a 'complex 9'.

To summarize the general point: The properties researchers are interested in measuring differ in the amount and complexity of the information they contain. Sometimes researchers are trying to capture differences in relatively simple information; at other times they are trying to capture differences in relatively complex information. The numbers used in a measurement can readily identify 'within class' differences (i.e., between objects of the same type). However, since digits are one-dimensional, they cannot tell us about 'between class differences'. So a system has been developed to distinguish the amount and complexity of the information captured by a measurement (i.e., between class differences). This system is called *levels of measurement*.

Levels of measurement

Imagine that a friend has asked for your help in hanging a picture on the wall. A small finishing nail is to be hammered into the wall to hold the picture, and you are asked to hold the nail between your thumb and forefinger in the correct location. Your friend leaves the room to get a tool for driving the small nail into the wall and returns, to your surprise, lugging a sledge hammer! Would you protest? Undoubtedly you would—on the grounds that the sledge hammer is the wrong tool for the job. A little nail requires a little hammer; a big job (like breaking a rock) calls for a big hammer.

Levels of measurement can be thought of in a parallel way. The different levels represent different 'tools'. In the case of levels of measurement, the tools differ in their ability to capture less or more sophisticated information. The lower levels of measurement are simple tools used to measure properties of objects that are not too sophisticated in their complexity. As you move up the levels of measurement, the tools become more sophisticated in that the measures they produce include more sophisticated information.

There are four levels of measurement, and as the name implies ('levels' of measurement), they can be ranked. From least to most sophisticated, these levels are known as nominal, ordinal, interval, and ratio, and their properties are as follows:

- *Nominal*: This is the lowest level, which means that the numbers provided by this level of measurement provide the least information. In fact, the numbers provided by nominal measures are not 'numbers' at all, since they do not provide any quantitative information. The 'numbers' used at this level of measurement are really replacements for 'names' (which, by the way, is what 'nominal' means). The only meaning the digits convey is that objects with the same number are equivalent and are *qualitatively* different from objects that have a different number. Think of the digits on a hockey player's jersey. The player who wears a 66 is not six times better than the player who wears 11. The number 66 simply serves as a substitute for the player's name. The scores of variables measured at the nominal level work the same way. The digits simply identify different categories of the variable (which is why nominal measures are sometimes called 'categorical' variables).
- *Ordinal*: Ordinal variables contain the same information as nominal variables, *plus some additional characteristic.* (This is the case because the various levels of measurement are 'nested' in one another—similar to those Russian stacked dolls, where every larger one contains all the ones that are smaller.) The additional characteristic possessed by ordinal measures is that the attributes of the variable can be *ranked* (i.e., ordered). In other words, the scores can be ranked from highest to lowest with respect to the measured property. The 5-point scale discussed earlier rating the statement about the prime minister's competence (1. strongly agree; 2. agree; 3. neutral; 4. disagree; 5. strongly disagree) exemplifies the ordinal level of measurement. The scale has a nominal property in that, for example, all respondents who score 4 have the same amount of agreement with the statement, and this amount differs from that of all those who score 1, 2, 3, or 5. The additional property that makes the scale ordinal is that respondents' scores can be ranked in terms of the 'intensity of their agreement' with the statement.
- *Interval*: The interval level of measurement starts with an ordinal measure and adds an important characteristic—which is that the distance between the various categories (i.e., the 'interval') is *fixed* or standardized. Note that this feature is absent from ordinal measures. If

runners are measured in terms of their place of finish in a race (e.g., first, second, third), we can rank their performance (which makes it ordinal)—but we *do not know* how much faster one finisher was than another. From the order of their finish we cannot tell whether the second-place finisher was a millisecond behind the winner or a minute behind. Interval measures, which use a fixed unit to indicate differences between categories, can provide the answer.

- *Ratio*: The highest level of measurement is ratio. Given the 'nested' nature of levels of measurement, the ratio level can be considered an 'interval plus'. The 'plus' provided by the ratio level of measurement is an *absolute zero point*. This contrasts with interval measures, which utilize an arbitrary zero. An arbitrary zero means that the original selection of what zero means could have been done for any reason whatsoever. For example, the Fahrenheit and Celsius temperature scales use arbitrary zeros. Anders Celsius decided to identify zero on his scale as the melting point of ice. Daniel Fahrenheit, on the other hand, chose to identify his zero point as the lowest temperature he could record in his lab by mixing together water, ice, and sea salt. This certainly qualifies as a whimsical choice of zero! By contrast, absolute zeros, which ratio levels of measurement use, literally mean *no amount* of the property under consideration. When the bank teller informs you that your bank balance is zero, this is not a capricious choice; it literally means that you have zero dollars in the account.

The following analogy may help you understand measurement more thoroughly. When researchers measure an object, they 'suck' information from it—as though they were drawing fluid into a sponge. The different levels of measurement indicate different amounts of 'fluid' (i.e., types and complexity of information). After measurement, the researcher now has the information stored—much like having a liquid-filled sponge in hand. At a later time (i.e., the statistical analysis stage), the researcher can wring the information out of the sponge for analysis purposes.

Some tips

The following points regarding the application of levels of measurement should be helpful:

- *Look at the actual attributes of the variable to determine level of measurement.* You cannot determine the level of measurement merely by looking at the name of the variable. Knowing that the variable is 'income' or 'intelligence' provides you with no clue about the level of measurement. The clue to determining levels of measurement is *the way the variable is scored* (i.e., its attributes or values). Look at them, and ask yourself: are the categories names only? (nominal); can the categories be ranked? (ordinal); is the difference between the categories fixed, and does it include an arbitrary zero? (interval); do the fixed differences between the categories include an absolute zero? (ratio).

- *Become thoroughly familiar with identifying levels of measurement.* The ability to identify levels of measurement will serve you well, since the selection of appropriate statistical analysis techniques is aligned with different levels of measurement. In other words, some analysis techniques are intended for nominal levels, others for ordinal, interval, or ratio levels. If you cannot identify the levels of measurement of your variables, you will experience endless problems with statistical selection. By contrast, knowing the levels of measurement of your variable(s) dramatically simplifies statistical analysis choices.

- *When you have a choice, you should always choose to measure objects at the highest legitimate level of measurement.*[1] This tip relates to the fact that levels of measurement are 'nested', which means that you can always go *down* the levels of measurement (i.e., you can always turn a ratio level into an interval one, an interval one into an ordinal one, and so on). Such reduction is possible because you are *simplifying* the information in the measure. If you have complex information, you can always simplify; however, if you begin by collecting too little information, you cannot later make it 'complex' (which is what moving *up* the levels of measurement would require).

LAB 4 APPLICATION

Learning objectives

The following lab questions are directed at helping you translate the tune-up points into concrete research situations. Specifically, this lab assignment challenges you to clarify your understanding of:

- the difference between ordinal and interval/ratio measures;
- the difference between interval and ratio measures;
- the characteristics of all levels of measurement.

Distinguishing ordinal from interval/ratio measures

Suppose that three runners competed in a 100 metre dash. Runner number 41 achieved first place; runner number 23 came second; and the third place runner was number 88. The following table indicates their places and times:

Place

#41:	1st place
#23:	2nd place
#88:	3rd place

Time

#41:	19.8 seconds
#23:	20.1 seconds
#88:	49.5 seconds

Explain how the information contained in this example illustrates the key difference between ordinal and interval/ratio levels of measurement.

_____

_____

_____

_____

Is the measure of the runners' time an interval or a ratio measure? How do you know?

Interval or ratio? _____

Justification: _____

_____

_____

Distinguishing interval and ratio measures

Suppose that you like to bake brownies every week. Sometimes you follow the recipe exactly (350° F for 30 minutes). Other times, you are in a hurry, so you bake them at a higher temperature for a shorter length of time. Still other times, you decide to bake them at a lower temperature for a longer length of time.

The table below outlines these three baking scenarios. For each situation, based on what you know about levels of measurement, describe the expected outcome in three or four words (i.e., state how the brownies would turn out under each of the baking scenarios).

Table 4.1

Temperature	Time in Oven	Outcome
350° F	30 minutes	
700° F	15 minutes	
175° F	60 minutes	

With reference to levels of measurement, explain your reasons for expecting the outcomes that you did. If you think that the outcome would be the same each time, why would you say so? Similarly, if you think it would differ, why?

_____

_____

_____

_____

Identifying levels of measurement and their characteristics

The following table lists 18 variables and specifies their values/attributes in parentheses. For each variable, check off those characteristics that exist in the measure and identify the variable's level of measurement.

Table 4.2

Variable	Equivalence within categories?	Ordered?	Fixed intervals?	Absolute zero?	Highest level of measurement
Religious preference (Protestant, Catholic)[2]					
Household income: Combined income of all members, to the nearest dollar ($10,000, $31,758)					
Unemployment rate: Percentage of the labour force unemployed (10.5%, 12.7%)					
Course rating: Overall student rating of course (average, good)					
Marital status (never married, married, divorced, widowed)					
Skin tone (light, medium, dark)					
Happiness: Rated on 7-point scale (1, 2, 3, 4, 5, 6, 7)					
Smoking status (non-smoker, occasional smoker, heavy smoker)					

Table 4.2 (continued)

Variable	Equivalence within categories?	Ordered?	Fixed intervals?	Absolute zero?	Highest level of measurement
Number of children in household (0, 1, 2, 3)[2]					
Number of times arrested (0, 1, 4, 15)					
Crime rate: Number of murders per 100,000 population (3, 4)					
Degree sought (BSc, MBA, PhD, BA, MD)					
IQ test score (120, 152)					
Church attendance (never or rarely, sometimes, often)					
Ethnicity (Chinese, Aboriginal)					
Favourite leisure activity (reading, watching TV)					
Grade in Introductory Sociology (A+, C)					
Tuition fees, to nearest dollar ($4,013, $8,880)					

A researcher uses the following survey question to measure the age of respondents. What level of measurement is this variable?

What is your age?

1. Under 25 years   (   )

2. 25–44 years   (   )

3. 45–64 years   (   )

5. 65 years or older   (   )

Level of measurement: _____

Justification: _____

_____

_____

The following question is used to determine a respondent's gender:

What is your gender?

1. Male   (   )

2. Female   (   )

Based on the information provided by this measurement, assess the reasonableness of the following propositions:

Males are the 'first' gender.

Reasonable or unreasonable? _____

Justification: _____

_____

_____

It takes two males to make up a female.

Reasonable or unreasonable? _____

Justification: _____

_____

_____

_____

On a 20-item vocabulary test, one respondent scores 14, and the other respondent scores 7. Based on the information provided by this measurement, assess the reasonableness of the following propositions:

The respondent who scored 14 provided two times as many correct answers as the respondent scoring 7.

Reasonable or unreasonable? _____

Justification: _____

_____

_____

_____

The respondent scoring 14 has twice as large a vocabulary as the respondent scoring 7.

Reasonable or unreasonable? _____

Justification: _____

_____

_____

_____

Note: Remember to consult the 'Tips for lab applications' section on the companion website (www.oupcanada.com/methodscoach) if you find you need help.

LAB 5
Quantitative Sampling Considerations

▶ Tune-up

Much of the subject matter of research methods can be sorted into answers to the following questions: What should we observe (sampling issues)? How should we observe it (measurement issues)? What other considerations are affecting our observations (design issues)? How do we appropriately summarize and interpret our findings (analysis issues)?

Collecting evidence rests on observing some 'thing'. The 'thing' may be persons (e.g., individuals), collectivities (e.g., nations), social artifacts (e.g., cartoons), or any of a myriad of concrete objects. However, whatever the objects of consideration, researchers are almost never in a situation in which they can observe all of the cases of interest. A quest to date *all* blondes to determine whether they have 'more fun' is doomed from the outset. Similarly, who would ever submit to a blood test that required donating *all* of one's blood? Enter sampling.

Sampling is the process of selecting, from the universe of *all* things (blondes, blood, nations, cartoons), which things should be observed. An extensive number of different sample procedures has been developed. Selecting the appropriate one depends on one's purpose.

The iron law of purpose

Nearly a century ago, the social scientist Robert Michels set forth his famous 'iron law of oligarchy'. Over the decades, other such ironclad laws governing human experience have emerged, one of which could well be labelled the 'iron law of purpose'. Although it can be simply stated, this law has far-reaching implications. Simply stated, the iron law of purpose declares that *you cannot evaluate anything without a conception of its purpose*.[1]

This succinct statement of the law is worth a short elaboration. Any act of evaluation requires an act of choosing, of deciding which alternative is preferable. The act of deciding, in turn, requires an assessment of the consequences of various alternatives. However, assessing consequences (outcomes) requires a prior conception of purpose. In short, without a conception of an object's purpose, you cannot assess its consequences. If you cannot assess an object's comparative consequences, you cannot evaluate its worth. This proposition can be labelled a 'law' because it *applies to everything*—from hammers to sweethearts, from vegetables to your life. If you are unclear on what anything is for (its purpose), then you cannot assess how worthwhile it is.

It follows, then, that we should apply this law when deciding which sampling procedure is appropriate for a given research problem. And we do.

A sample's purpose

When a researcher is deciding which objects to observe (i.e., what type of sample to select), the question of the sample's purpose arises. A basic distinction among sampling purposes concerns whether (or not) it is important to be able to *calculate how representative the sample's findings are.* Samples always involve selecting some objects from all objects of a particular type. If it is important to estimate how likely it is that the sample objects reflect the population of objects, then researchers look to *probability sampling* techniques. If this purpose is not paramount, then researchers often look to *non-probability sampling* techniques. As always, the choice of a specific kind of sample requires that one be clear about primary objectives.[2]

Non-probability samples

In non-probability samples, the likelihood of selecting a particular member of the population into the sample is unknown. Non-probability sampling is commonly used in research projects with a qualitative focus. These projects typically utilize smaller sample sizes and are interested in gaining a more intensive understanding of some specific cases or processes. Imagine that you wanted to provide a narrative about self-images and interaction in an Aboriginal community, or tell the stories of two contrasting fishing communities, or explore how members are recruited into a cult.[3] In these cases, you would be interested in intensively exploring the uniqueness of the cases under consideration. Such a purpose does not require numbers, statistics, or generalizations and therefore requires a different type of sampling. Non-probability samples are designed for just such purposes.

There are a wide variety of non-probability sampling procedures, some of which are outlined below.

- Haphazard sampling: As the name indicates, this type of sample selects participants on an accidental or convenience basis. It is a favourite technique on radio and TV news programs with their person-on-the-street interviews and web polls.
- Purposive sampling: In this sampling technique, specific participants are selected deliberately on the basis of how strongly they typify features of interest. Optimally, this sampling procedure is used when researchers have the expertise to judge what kind of cases are worthy of intensive investigation (e.g., in selecting a sample of elderly persons with AIDS).
- Network sampling: This is sometimes called the 'snowball' method, since it relies on asking initial participants to recruit others. This method is particularly useful when a researcher is trying to expand a sample in a group with unusual characteristics (e.g., chief executives of major corporations).
- Deviant case sampling: It is often instructive to examine the outer limits of a phenomenon of interest, and deviant case sampling involves selecting such extreme cases for intensive examination. For example, in areas where the educational achievement of Aboriginal students is

generally low, an examination of schools where Aboriginals have achieved remarkable success can yield constructive insights.

These are only a few of the large number of non-probability sampling procedures that qualitative researchers use to achieve their purposes.[4] The important point is what those purposes are. Because researchers' purposes vary so widely, non-probability sampling techniques do not follow a standard set of methodologies or techniques. Each technique has its own place, procedures, and purpose.

Probability samples

In contrast to the diversity and idiosyncrasies of non-probability sampling techniques, probability samples are rooted in a set of common denominators. These common denominators relate to the fact that all probability samples are aimed at making inferences about a general case from a set of specific cases.

Probability samples derive their name from the fact that the likelihood (probability) of any member of the population (all objects of interest) being selected into the sample is known. When population members have an equal probability of being selected into the sample, then some type of random sampling procedure is being used.

Probability sampling is most commonly used in quantitative research projects. Quantitative projects typically utilize larger sample sizes and are aimed at an accurate generalization of the results. Whereas non-probability samples are used to explore the idiosyncratic through narratives and stories, probability samples are used for generalizing through numbers and statistics.

There are various types of probability samples, some of which are sketched below.

- *Simple random sampling*: This type of probability sample is less often used, but it is the prototype for other techniques. It involves identifying a full set of elements and then using some random procedure (e.g., a table of random numbers) for selecting the sample. Although ideal in theory, this method presents challenges in practice. Principal among these challenges is how to identify the full set of elements (for example, where would you get a complete, up-to-date, accurate list of all adults in Canada?) and how to cost-effectively contact those who are chosen.
- *Systematic sampling*: This procedure is based on simple random sampling, but instead of repeatedly drawing random elements, the researcher uses a random entry point and a sampling interval. The sampling interval is a fraction generated by dividing the population size by the desired sample size. For example, if the population contains 10,000 elements and you want a sample of 100, then the sampling interval would be 100. With the sampling interval calculated, the first case is selected randomly, and then every 100th case after that is chosen for inclusion in the sample. Systematic sampling improves on the efficiency of sample selection but has its own challenges (especially if there is periodicity in the list, such as every 100th element sharing some odd characteristic).

- *Stratified sampling*: This more refined method of probability sampling begins with the identification of categories within the population that are distinct on the basis of some criterion and relevant to the researcher's purpose. Let's take religion as an example. If a random sample is drawn from a population, it is highly unlikely that there will be enough cases of Muslims, Jews, Christians, and Buddhists to make meaningful comparisons. In such an instance, it would be better for the researcher to initially 'stratify' the sample by religion and then randomly select from within each stratum (subgroup).
- *Cluster sampling*: This method is commonly used when researchers do not have complete lists of elements (for example, where would you find a list of all Canadian high school students?) or when cost-effective data collection is important. The idea of cluster sampling is to sample in stages. The first stage is typically to sample a large unit, such as schools or geographical regions. In our example, we could initially select a random list of Canadian high schools. The next stage is to sample within the selected units (e.g., randomly select students within the selected high schools). This makes the sample much more geographically concentrated so that the researcher does not have to travel across the country interviewing students.

As with non-probability samples, there are a large number of sophisticated variations on these fundamental probability sampling types. But in one form or another, they are all intended to make generalizations possible, which they achieve through a shared set of tools.

Sampling distributions

Sampling distribution is a key tool in probability sampling and essential in making inferences. Note that almost all inferential research is conducted on a single probability sample. But no matter what probability sampling procedure is used, it is risky to rely on a single sample. Imagine that you want to estimate the average income of individuals in your community. You put the names of all the adults into a hat, randomly draw a sample of 100 names, and calculate the average income. In any one sample (which is what researchers use), there is some chance that the result will be atypical. You could, for example, randomly draw the 100 richest (or 100 poorest) people in your community, and that would give you your estimate of 'average'.

The point is that probability sampling does not guarantee representativeness. At best, it only makes representativeness more likely. The crucial question, then, is estimating *how likely* the sample results are to be representative.

Estimating how likely a particular sample's results are representative relies on a crucial tool called a sampling distribution. Discussions of sampling distributions involve many technical considerations, but the central consideration is as follows: If you repeatedly draw samples and plot the results, *the greater the number of samples, the more closely the results will approximate a normal distribution*. This is a critical point, because generalizations from samples would otherwise be impossible.

LAB 5 APPLICATION

Learning objectives

The following lab questions are directed at helping you translate the tune-up points into concrete research situations. Specifically, this lab assignment challenges you to clarify your understanding that:

- qualitative and quantitative studies have different sampling purposes;
- different probability sampling techniques serve different goals;
- the principle underlying sampling distributions creates normality.

Sampling purposes

Imagine that you know nothing about homelessness but want to understand what it is like to be a homeless person in a large city. Which of the four types of non-probability samples highlighted in the tune-up would be most appropriate for your purposes? Justify your choice.

Sample type: _____

Justification: _____

_____

_____

_____

_____

Probability Sampling

Sampling decision

The solicitor general's department intends to conduct a Canadian study comparing the characteristics of prisoners who attempt to commit suicide with those who do not. They have just learned that their budget for this investigation has been cut by half. Consequently, they cannot afford to use a simple random sampling procedure. Given their situation, *identify* and *justify* an alternative sampling technique that they could use.

_____

_____

_____

_____

_____

Sampling alternatives

Imagine that you want to study the quality of life of students in the Faculty of Arts. For each of the following two sampling alternatives, (i) provide a brief statement of what is required in order to draw the sample, (ii) how it would be drawn, and (iii) the likely disadvantages of the procedure.

Simple random sample

   i. Requirements:

_____

_____

_____

  ii. Procedures:

_____

_____

_____

iii. Disadvantages:

_____

_____

_____

Stratified sample

   i. Requirements:

_____

_____

_____

ii. Procedures:

_____

_____

_____

iii. Disadvantages:

_____

_____

_____

Sampling distributions

Tossing coins

Sampling distributions plot the results of a large number of samples. A central principle underlying sampling distributions (and therefore the ability to generalize on the basis of probability samples) is that sampling distributions will approximate a normal distribution, as the following exercise demonstrates.

Collect six coins, all of the same value (e.g., all quarters, all nickels). If you toss all the coins into the air and let them fall, you will obtain some 'results' from your sample. Let's say that the result of interest is the 'number of heads' that appear among the six coins. Repeat the coin-tossing exercise 200 times, each time recording the number of heads among the six coins (use the table below).

Table 5.1

Toss #	# Heads	Toss #	# Heads	Toss #	# Heads	Toss #	# Heads
1		51		101		151	
2		52		102		152	
3		53		103		153	
4		54		104		154	
5		55		105		155	
6		56		106		156	
7		57		107		157	
8		58		108		158	
9		59		109		159	
10		60		110		160	

Table 5.1 (continued)

Toss #	# Heads	Toss #	# Heads	Toss #	# Heads	Toss #	# Heads
11		61		111		161	
12		62		112		162	
13		63		113		163	
14		64		114		164	
15		65		115		165	
16		66		116		166	
17		67		117		167	
18		68		118		168	
19		69		119		169	
20		70		120		170	
21		71		121		171	
22		72		122		172	
23		73		123		173	
24		74		124		174	
25		75		125		175	
26		76		126		176	
27		77		127		177	
28		78		128		178	
29		79		129		179	
30		80		130		180	
31		81		131		181	
32		83		132		182	
33		83		133		183	
34		84		134		184	
35		85		135		185	
36		86		136		186	
37		87		137		187	

Table 5.1 (continued)

Toss #	# Heads	Toss #	# Heads	Toss #	# Heads	Toss #	# Heads
38		88		138		188	
39		89		139		189	
40		90		140		190	
41		91		141		191	
42		92		142		192	
43		93		143		193	
44		94		144		194	
45		95		145		195	
46		96		146		196	
47		97		147		197	
48		98		148		198	
49		99		149		199	
50		100		150		200	

You have now obtained the results (i.e., number of heads) from repeated samples (200). If you plot these results, you will create a sampling distribution. In the space below, create a simple bar graph of your results, with the 'number of heads' as the horizontal axis (ranging from 0 to 6) and the 'number of events' as the vertical axis.

Figure 5.1 200 sample results

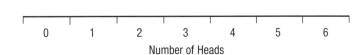

Does the sampling distribution you have created approximate a normal (bell-shaped) distribution? How do you know?

_____

_____

_____

Most people would find it unusual if they tossed six coins and all six came up 'heads' or all came up 'tails'. Based on your results, how likely is each of these events?

All heads occurs _____ per cent of the time.

All tails occurs _____ per cent of the time.

Increasing cases

In theory, a sampling distribution becomes perfectly 'normal' in shape when the results of an _infinite_ number of samples have been plotted. In the coin-tossing exercise, you plotted the results for 200 cases. It should be the case that as your sampling distribution includes progressively more sample results, it will become more normal in shape.

To test this idea, let's create different sampling distributions based on progressively larger numbers of cases. In the space below, create a bar graph of the same format you used previously. This time, however, include the results of _only the first 5 coin tosses_.

Figure 5.2 First 5 sample results

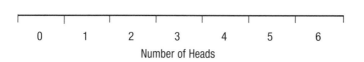

Now create a graph of the first 10 coin tosses.

Figure 5.3 First 10 sample results

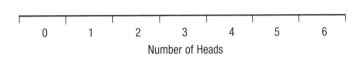

Number of Heads

Now create a graph of the first 50 coin tosses.

Figure 5.4 First 50 sample results

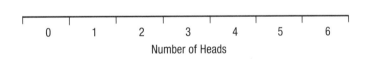

Number of Heads

Now create a graph of the first 100 coin tosses.

Figure 5.5 First 100 sample results

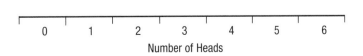

Number of Heads

Earlier you plotted the graph of 200 coin tosses. So as a final attempt, create a graph of 350 coin tosses. Rather than having you toss the coins another 150 times, we have conducted 150 trials on your behalf. The cells in the table below contain the number of heads in each trial.

Table 5.2   Outcomes of 150 additional trials

1	3	1	1	0	3	3	5
4	4	3	3	2	4	4	6
3	4	3	3	4	1	2	2
2	3	3	1	2	4	2	3
5	1	3	4	1	1	3	1
4	4	2	5	3	2	4	3
2	1	2	3	2	4	2	3
1	2	2	4	2	4	3	5
3	4	4	3	1	3	4	1
5	3	2	5	3	5	2	2
4	5	1	3	4	3	2	
3	4	2	1	3	4	2	
4	2	2	3	3	5	2	
6	3	3	3	0	4	3	
3	2	3	3	2	4	3	
3	2	2	3	3	1	2	
2	3	2	4	1	3	3	
4	3	2	3	3	2	4	
2	1	3	2	2	3	4	
5	4	5	3	5	2	4	

Figure 5.6 350 sample results

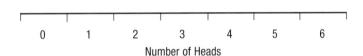

Now look at the shape of the graphs you created for the 5, 10, 50, 100, 200, and 350 sample results.

Do the graphs take a progressively more 'normal' shape?

_____

_____

We know that if you randomly flip a coin, there is a 50 per cent chance it will come up heads. Therefore, if you flip six coins simultaneously, how many of them should come up heads?

_____

Calculate the percentage of times three heads occur in each of the six sampling distributions you created. Record your results below.

Table 5.3

Number of cases	Percentage of three heads
5	
10	
50	
100	
200	
350	

Do your results provide progressively better approximations of the theoretically anticipated 'three heads' results?

_____

_____

What does this exercise tell you about the credibility of sampling distributions that underlie probability sampling inferences?

_____

_____

Note: Remember to consult the 'Tips for lab applications' section on the companion website (www.oupcanada.com/methodscoach) if you find you need help.

LAB 6
Survey Design Issues

▶ Tune-up

Prevalence of surveys

As previously demonstrated, asking people questions of interest does not result in perfect answers. Nonetheless, surveys, which are rooted in such question-asking, continue to be the most widely used data collection method in the social sciences. Howard Schuman, one of the gurus in the field, explains the enduring prevalence of surveys this way: 'Surveys remain our best tool for learning about large populations. . . . one remarkable advantage surveys have over some other methods is the ability to identify their own limitations.'[1]

The identification of common errors that limit the method's credibility is perhaps more established in survey research than in other data collection strategies. In survey research, most design errors are of one of two types: *question design* errors and *questionnaire format* errors.

Question design errors

This category of errors involves mistakes in the way questions are *asked*. Such common errors include:

1. *Questions requiring overly specific responses and therefore coming across as threatening or otherwise objectionable.* At root, asking people questions is a human encounter. (Witness the great resistance and resentment people exhibit toward market researchers who intrude into their private time and space!) It is important that questions not be so specific (either in their form or in the responses they require) that respondents feel threatened (imagine, for example, questions about drug consumption, sexual habits, or income).
2. *Questions that permit recall bias.* To varying degrees (and that degree can be outstanding), we all have faulty memories. Therefore, when respondents are asked about events in the past, they are not likely to remember them accurately in specific detail. Errors become more likely the more distant the memory becomes.
3. *Response categories that lack mutual exclusiveness and/or exhaustiveness.* For closed-ended questions (i.e., those for which the response categories are provided), the array of possible responses must meet these two criteria. In other words, there must be a response category for each possible response (exhaustiveness), and each response must fit into only one category

(mutual exclusiveness). If that is not the case, the respondents' confusion will confound the exercise.

4. *Vague or ambiguous language.* Vague terms are those that do not have clear referents; ambiguous terms are those that have multiple referents. Designers of survey questions often wrongly assume that respondents have vocabularies equivalent to their own, forgetting that a majority of the general public does not have the benefit of extensive education. Therefore, you should examine all the terms in a question, including both the question or statement and the responses. Ask yourself whether a clerk at your local supermarket would have a clear idea of what the concepts mean. If not, then rewrite the entry using simple, clear language.

5. *Questions that assume too much knowledge.* The general public's understanding of many topics can be surprisingly narrow. (One recent survey reported that the most popular reading material was *People* magazine and *TV Guide*!) Therefore, it is risky to assume a high level of knowledge when drafting a survey question, since many respondents may not be familiar with the topic (for example, the names of and details about particular social policies or programs). First examine each question and determine whether it refers to current, widely known events or to other issues. Then ask yourself whether it is reasonable to assume that the proverbial supermarket employee would be knowledgeable about the subject. If not, then something has to be done to improve the question. Some possibilities include: (i) providing a short statement that describes the issue before asking the question; (ii) adding a question asking respondents the extent of their knowledge about the issue (and then providing a 'skip' for respondents who are inadequately informed); and (iii) providing a response category allowing respondents to declare their lack of knowledge.

6. *Questions that include a double negative.* Your grade school English and arithmetic teachers probably taught you that 'a double negative is the same as a positive.' Although this is true, such constructions are confusing. (Imagine your sweetheart telling you, 'I don't dislike you.') To prevent unnecessary confusion, survey questions need to avoid double negatives. See whether your question contains negative words like 'not' or 'no'. If it does, look carefully to see whether the construction is a double negative. If it is, rewrite the question in positive terms. You might initially try deleting the 'not' from the statement and see what effect that has.

7. *Loaded questions.* In this context, 'loaded' questions are those that include biased language that can shape the respondent's attitude (for example, 'crisis', 'terrible', 'deplorable'). Examine questions and remove any such 'loading'.

8. *Leading questions.* Leading questions contain an assumption about the respondent's attitude and, in doing so, limit (bias) the response. For example, you might ask me: 'Have you quit beating your dog?' Whether I answer 'yes' or 'no', I am constrained from reporting my actual conduct, which is that I do not beat my dog. Leading questions can be tricky to spot. Read each question carefully, and ask yourself what assumptions are built into it. Such assumptions may bias the responses. One way to manage the issue is to begin with a question that specifies the topic under assumption—for example, 'In the past, have you beaten your dog?'

9. *Double-barrelled questions.* When a double-barrelled shotgun is fired, it produces twice the blast of a single-barrelled gun. This is a desirable effect if you want to cover a lot of territory.

Too often, question designers impatiently 'blast' respondents with more than one question (or response) simultaneously. These are double-barrelled questions. Double-barrelled questions create problems because it is not clear which component(s) of the question the respondent is answering. Because they cause severe problems for interpretation, double-barrelled questions are to be avoided. A common clue to the presence of double-barrelling is the use of the word 'and' in either the question or the response category—for example, 'Do you like the textbook and coming to class?' To clear up double-barrelled questions, reduce the 'blast'—i.e., separate the question into its component parts either by asking separate questions or by providing distinct response categories.

Questionnaire format errors

This category of errors involves mistakes in the way questions are structured on a survey. Here are some common errors of this type:

1. *Starting the survey with questions that are unlikely to capture the respondent's interest.* People lead busy lives, and answering survey questions is probably not high on their list of priorities. So it is counterproductive for researchers to exaggerate this attitude by reducing interest in their project. Accordingly, whenever possible, surveys should begin with questions that are more (rather than less) interesting. This is why socio-demographic questions (e.g., sex, age, marital status) should be asked at the end of a survey.

2. *Inserting questions that are irrelevant to the theme of a particular section of the survey.* As noted earlier, it is a fact (not an evaluation) that the general public is not well-practised in sophisticated cognitive work. Survey researchers should assume that potential respondents are easily distracted and confused. Therefore, it is important to group survey questions into 'themes' whenever possible. Themes help respondents to appreciate the coherence of the project and keep them focused. For this reason, questions of a similar type should appear together on a survey.

3. *Violating or questioning anonymity.* With rare exceptions, surveys are meant to gather aggregated evidence rather than the particular views of a specific respondent. The typical goal of survey work is to generalize about some population—for example, to estimate the average hours worked per week or the average amount of marijuana smoked. Consequently, to encourage participation, respondents are guaranteed anonymity (or at least confidentiality). Asking questions that violate or question the premise of respondent anonymity (such as asking their name or place of employment) is not helpful and typically results in lower response rates.

4. *Not including instructions on how to respond to a question or questions.* As noted earlier, it is risky to assume too much of respondents. They are generally unfamiliar with survey techniques and therefore need to be guided. Unless it is really obvious, respondents need to be directed about how to report their answers. (Note that such direction is very different from shaping their opinions.) For example, if they are permitted to give more than one appropriate response, you must make this explicit. Are they supposed to circle or check their preferred response?

5. *Inattention to attribute scoring.* Remember that respondents probably have better things to do (certainly in their own view) than complete a survey. Consequently, it is unreasonable to assume that you will have their undivided attention. Much of the time, respondents may behave as though they were on some form of 'automatic pilot'. Given this common state of mind, it is worthwhile to order and score attributes in some intuitively sensible manner. For example, if the responses are supposed to increase in intensity, then the scores of the attributes should also increase.

6. *Insensitivity to the way that 'order effects' may bias answers.* Questions raise respondents' awareness of issues. When awareness is raised, answers to subsequent questions (especially those immediately following a question) may be contaminated. Such potential contamination is called 'order effects'. For example, if a survey asks about the level of crime in a community and then about attitudes toward punishment, it is likely that the latter will be exaggerated.

7. *Changing response formats.* To avoid confusion and the errors that follow or, worse, respondent withdrawal, response formats should be as consistent as possible. For example, all response alternatives might be listed vertically. Inconsistencies in response format (e.g., alternating between vertical and horizontal) can create confusion.

8. *Inappropriate or inadequate 'skip' instructions.* Some questions should only be answered if a previous question was answered a particular way. For example, it is not appropriate to ask for a rating of the quality of marriage if the respondent is single. If a contingent question is inappropriate, it should be skipped, and instructions need to indicate this direction. If the skip instructions are inappropriate or inadequate, then the data will contain a number of inappropriate responses.

9. *Providing inadequate space to answer.* Some questions are best left 'open-ended', which means that the possible response categories are not predetermined. When this is the case and respondents are asked to provide open-ended (written) commentary, they need to have adequate space to do so. Leaving just a line or two for a response to a challenging question only contributes to respondent cynicism about the survey's sincerity.

Precision versus accuracy

Professional sports can play an important social function, but they can also contain many absurdities. A recent Canadian Football League game provided one such instance. A running back charged through the line and was met by a mass of humanity. He was tackled, and when the referee's whistle blew, there was literally a ton of flesh on top of him. You could hardly see the tackled player, and there was no sign of the ball within the pile. However, the pile was progressively sorted out, and then the referee placed the ball on a precise spot—as though he knew exactly where the ball had been underneath the pile! To complete the absurd ritual, the crew that controlled the first-down distance markers was brought onto the field, and when the measurement was complete, the ball was determined to be about 2.54 centimetres short of the first-down mark. The players on the field and the fans in the stands had no problem with the official ruling.

Now, of course, football would degenerate into madness if this measurement system were seriously challenged. It is considered just part of the game. But we all know that the system is flawed: a referee has only a vague idea of where the ball actually should be placed.

What this example illustrates is the trade-off between 'precision' and 'accuracy'. Precision refers to the fineness of the distinctions captured in an action or answer. More precise answers are more specific. Precision is a virtue, but it is a virtue that comes at a cost. In the everyday world (as opposed to CFL football!), gaining more precision generally requires more resources. Because additional precision requires the expenditure of additional resources, as a general rule, survey research questions are designed to capture only the level of precision required; anything more wastes valuable resources.

Measurement accuracy is a separate but related matter. Accuracy refers to the correctness of an answer. More accurate answers are by definition more desirable.

Since both precision and accuracy are desirable, it would seem reasonable to want to maximize both in the answers to questions. However, trying to do so creates a serious problem: *Any attempt to maximize precision can compromise accuracy.* In other words, if we aim for too much precision, the answers risk becoming less correct.

How much money did you spend last month on all your expenses? If you have to answer to the nearest $1,000, you will probably be quite accurate but not very precise. If you answer to the nearest $100, you become more precise but risk accuracy. If you answer to the nearest penny, your response will be very precise but very likely inaccurate.

The lesson: Asking questions requires that you be sensitive to the trade-offs between the precision and the accuracy of answers. Your goal should be to find an optimal amount (i.e., enough) of each feature rather than to 'maximize' (i.e., obtain all) of each feature.

LAB 6 APPLICATION

Learning objectives

The following lab questions are directed at helping you translate the tune-up points into concrete research situations. Specifically, this lab assignment challenges you to clarify your understanding of:

- question design errors;
- questionnaire format errors;
- trade-offs between precision and accuracy.

Identifying survey flaws

The following pages contain a health and health opinions survey. It is replete with errors. Your task is to *identify at least 10 different types of survey flaws* in this instrument. Please note that this task involves identifying different *types*. It is not enough to identify 10 errors of the same type in the survey (e.g., 10 instances of ambiguous wording). Rather, you are looking for different types of flaws.

You should feel free to *identify any error by making notes on the survey* itself. Note, however, that you *need to be specific*. It is not enough to say, for example, that 'this question is confusing.' You need to specify exactly *why* it is confusing.

Medical Attitudes Provincial Survey (MAPS)
Your Health and Health Opinions

Your Opinion Matters!

Your household has been randomly selected from a list of addresses in the provincial telephone books. We are a team of university researchers interested in understanding how people feel about their health and health care. <u>The more knowledge that researchers have about health matters, the more easily we can improve our health care system in your province.</u> Please take a few minutes to answer the questions in this booklet.

SURVEY INSTRUCTIONS: Please select the household head (who must be aged 18+) to answer every question by checking one box '□' or filling in the blank where appropriate. If you are unsure about how to answer a question, please give the best answer you can.

Your participation is voluntary. Because we realize that your privacy is very important, **all of your answers will remain anonymous**. If you have any questions about this booklet, please call Dr Jean Scott at 1-800-474-MAPS (extension 6377).

When you have completed the booklet, please fold it, place it in the self-addressed, stamped envelope provided, and drop it into any mailbox within **30 days** from today. In order to protect your anonymity, please do not write your name or return address on the envelope. The postmark will indicate the part of the province in which you live, but otherwise you cannot be personally identified to us or anyone else.

> University Health Research Group Council

First of all, we would like to know a little bit about you so that we can learn about the health and opinions of different types of people.

1. What is your sex?

Male ....□
Female ....□

2. What is your age range?

18–35 ....□
35–55 ....□
55–64 ....□
65 and over ....□

3. What is your current marital status?

Never legally married ....□
Legally married (and not separated) ....□
Separated but still legally married ....□
Divorced ....□
Widowed ....□

4. Do you believe that it is morally wrong for people to live common-law? ('Common-law' refers to two people of the opposite sex or of the same sex who live together as a couple but who are not legally married to each other.)

Yes ....□
No ....□

(continued...)

Improving survey questions

Winston Churchill (or some such sage figure) once noted that 'It is easy to tell what's wrong. It is telling what's right that's difficult.' This dictum applies to surveys: creating constructive survey questions is often more difficult than it appears.

Below are three survey questions. The first two come from the survey you have just reviewed, the third from an actual market research opinion poll.

Your task is to create *improved versions* of each of these questions. Below your improved version, *explain why* your version is better than the original.

Opinion on health care

Original: *Do you think that the Canadian health care crisis would not improve if we had a new federal minister of health?*

Yes ....□
No ....□

Improved version:

_____

_____

_____

_____

_____

Explanation for improvement:

_____

_____

_____

_____

_____

Opinion on harm reduction

Original: *Do you support harm reduction programs like the one in Vancouver?* [2]

Yes ....□
No ....□

Improved version:

_____

_____

_____

_____

_____

Explanation for improvement:

_____

_____

_____

_____

_____

Opinion on automobile insurance rates

Original: *On a 5-point scale where 1 means 'strongly disagree' and 5 means 'strongly agree', how would you respond to the following statement:*

> *My automobile insurance company is doing a good job*
> *at maintaining stable and fair rates.*

Improved version:

_____

_____

_____

_____

Explanation for improvement:

_____

_____

_____

_____

Precision versus accuracy

Problems in surveys are not confined to question and design flaws. Often, the precision versus accuracy issue arises when making choices about the optimal *format* for questions. A common instance of this issue involves the choice between using open- versus closed-ended questions. Below are two options for a telephone survey question related to the issue of income.

Option A: Open-ended version

What is your annual income? That is, what is your total personal income before taxes from all sources, such as employment, pensions, and investments? (RECORD VERBATIM)

$

Option B: Closed-ended version

What is your total annual personal income before taxes from all sources, such as employment, pensions, and investments? Please stop me when I read the figure that comes closest to your total income.

1. Less than $20,000
2. $20,000–39,999
3. $40,000–59,999
4. $60,000–79,999
5. $80,000–99,999
6. $100,000 or more
7. Don't know (DO NOT PROMPT)
8. No response (DO NOT PROMPT)

Think about the issues surrounding the use of very personal questions, threatening questions, or questions requiring a detailed recall of events. In particular, consider whether or not such questions are likely to create a non-response bias (e.g., refusal to answer) or a response bias (such as deliberately giving an inaccurate response).

Given what you know about these issues, to what extent would each of the two options illustrated above provide *accuracy* and *precision*? For each of the two options, *circle the answer* below that best characterizes it in terms of the accuracy and precision of the results it would likely generate. In the space below each option, *explain* your choice.

Option A (open-ended version):

a. higher accuracy, lower precision
b. lower accuracy, higher precision
c. lower accuracy, lower precision
d. higher accuracy, higher precision

Explanation for choice:

_____

_____

_____

_____

_____

Option B (closed-ended version):

a. higher accuracy, lower precision
b. lower accuracy, higher precision
c. lower accuracy, lower precision
d. higher accuracy, higher precision

Explanation for choice:

_____

_____

_____

_____

_____

Note: Remember to consult the 'Tips for lab applications' section on the companion website (www.oupcanada.com/methodscoach] if you find you need help.

LAB 7
Content Analysis: Instrument Pre-testing

▶ Tune-up

Surveys are the social science data collection method best known to the general public. Almost everyone has been solicited to participate in some kind of survey. For those who have had their dinners and evenings repeatedly disrupted by telemarketers' survey requests, contact with surveys has probably been too extensive.

This lab, and the two following ones, shift the focus to a less-known but important methodological approach. This method is called content analysis.

Cases

Evidence to test an idea is collected from 'some thing'. In research, the 'thing' that is the object of attention is called a case. A case is the subject from which observations (measurements) are collected. In the social sciences, the most common association of 'case' is individuals or aggregations related to individuals such as groups, communities, and nations.

Cases, however, can also include the *products* of human experience. In other words, cases can include human 'artifacts'. Artifacts include all the materials generated by humans, from cooking utensils, through musical instruments, to transportation forms. As archeology demonstrates, a great deal about people and their way of life can be learned by studying the artifacts that remain after they have left the scene.

Content analysis is a method for analyzing and learning from a special type of artifact. Specifically, content analysis techniques are typically applied to artifacts related to *human communication*. Such communication may be spoken, written, or pictorial and may cover an extensive array of items such as books, newspapers, diaries, interview transcripts, television programs, and films.

Variables and their content

One distinctive feature of content analysis is that it widens the range of objects that can be the targets of systematic investigation. It does so by broadening the focus from individuals and their social systems to artifacts that are the concrete products of human activity. But this shift in focus does not fundamentally alter the research approach. We are still concerned with identifying, measuring, and analyzing the *variable properties* of communication artifacts.

Variables are 'properties of objects that can change'. The range of possible amounts of the property measured by a variable are its 'attributes'. One way of appreciating the uniqueness of any object is to identify its constellation of attributes on a set of variables. For example, what makes any person unique is that he or she is a 'certain amount' (attribute) of age, height, introversion, blood type, social class, and so on (variables). In a parallel way, an artifact of human communication (e.g., a newspaper) can be measured and analyzed in terms of its unique combination of variable attributes.

The attributes of a variable are that specific variable's 'content'. Likewise, the 'content' (i.e., composition) of any artifact is its attributes (scores) across a range of variables. Using this viewpoint provides an appreciation of what the technique of content analysis entails. Content analysis is a methodological technique for gathering, summarizing, and interpreting information about the artifacts of communication. The information utilized in content analysis comes from scoring (i.e., identifying the attributes of) the artifacts on a set of variables.

Coding

The collection of evidence through content analysis centres on a process called coding. Coding involves the examination of an artifact and scoring it on the variables of interest. In other words, coding involves measuring an artifact by assigning it scores on relevant variables.

Technically, coding involves translating content from one format (language) into another. In the case of content analysis, the content of an artifact is translated into numerical form. The term 'numerical form' means that the attributes of each variable are represented by numbers, so scoring an artifact on a particular variable involves assigning it a number. For example, one variable on which newspapers differ is their amount of advertising. Amount of advertising might be measured in terms of the percentage of a newspaper's pages devoted to advertising. Various newspapers could be measured on this variable by assigning each of them their appropriate score.

The process of coding utilizes variables. Good-quality variables have attributes that meet two criteria, mutual exclusiveness and exhaustiveness. The attributes of a variable are mutually exclusive when the categories do not overlap. This property ensures that the object being measured can only be assigned a single score. The attributes of a variable are exhaustive when they cover all possible scores. This property ensures that all objects can be assigned a score on the variable.

Assigning codes

In a survey, when a subject either is interviewed or completes a survey, the subject is *providing the codes* for the variables of interest. For example, imagine a person being asked the following question: 'On a 7-point scale of increasing agreement, how would you rate your attitude toward the statement: *The professor of my class is exceptional*?' When the respondent reports their attitude as a 6, they are coding themselves. This kind of result occurs with self-report data.

In content analysis, the situation is different, since the artifacts of communication (e.g., diaries, newspapers, films) do not 'speak for themselves'. A newspaper can no more tell you what percentage of its pages are devoted to advertising than a film can tell you what its moral message is. Therefore, in content analysis, the *onus is on the researcher to examine the artifact's content and assign it scores*.

Pre-testing

Measuring the content of communication artifacts in terms of variables is challenging. Two challenges are of particular relevance. The first is to ensure that the attributes of the variables are properly specified (i.e., that they are mutually exclusive and exhaustive). The second challenge is to ensure reliability (consistency) in the way that the content is translated into numerical codes. Although researchers set up their variables and guidelines as carefully as possible, there is no way of knowing how adequate content analysis procedures are until they conduct a pre-test.

A pre-test is a kind of trial run that serves two purposes. The first purpose is to provide the researcher with feedback on how adequately the variables are specified and how reliably they are being measured. The second purpose is to give coders (those who are measuring the artifact's content) an opportunity to practise applying the measurement categories.

On the basis of information provided by the pre-test, the researcher can make improvements to either the measurement instrument or the coders' techniques.

LAB 7 APPLICATION

Learning objectives

The following lab questions are directed at helping you translate the tune-up points into concrete research situations. Specifically, this lab assignment challenges you to clarify your understanding of:

- the nature of content analysis coding;
- how coding is actually conducted;
- the challenges involved in creating good-quality variables for coding.

The content

A salient fact of social life in modern societies is the prevalence of mass communication. This lab focuses on a pervasive form of mass communication—advertising. Advertising is directed at influencing people's attitudes and motivations, whether for economic, political, social, educational, or other reasons. Some advertising, of course, is better than others.

This lab uses television commercials that have been touted as among the world's best. The selection of television commercials you are using for this lab is available from the website associated with the text (www.oupcanada.com/methodscoach). The specific commercials are under the headings 'Pre-test Commercials 1' and 'Pre-test Commercials 2'.

Data recording sheet

In this content analysis, you will be coding the content of the television commercials. Before proceeding to view and score the commercials, you need two things. The first requirement is a 'data recording sheet'. The data recording sheet provides you with a *place* to *record* your scores on the relevant variables in an *organized* manner. Here is an example of what the top of a data recording sheet looks like.

Table 7.1   Sample data recording sheet

ID	Product type	Sex of main character	Instances of violence	Humour rating	Quality rating	Main event
1	1. Alcohol 2. Food/bev. 3. Sports 4. Grooming 5. Autos 6. Other	1. Male 2. Female	(record actual number)	1. Not funny 2. 3. 4. 5. Very funny	1. Very low 2. 3. 4. 5. Very high	(write in your own words)

Note that the *columns* of the data recording sheet identify the *variables* that are to be coded. In this case, television commercials will be coded in terms of their product type, sex of the main character, instances of violence, humour, quality, and main event. Below the listing of the variable in each column are the variable's *attributes*, which identify the *possible scores* on which any commercial can be measured. For example, the humour of a commercial can be given any score between 1 and 5, with 1 meaning 'not funny' and 5 meaning 'very funny'.

The *rows* of the data recording sheet provide the *place* for you to score each commercial on each of the variables. Each row is allocated to a separate commercial. Therefore, a full data recording sheet will contain *as many rows as there are commercials* to be scored. Here is what a completed data recording sheet might look like for a *single* commercial:

Table 7.2   Sample completed data recording sheet

ID	Product type	Sex of main character	Instances of violence	Humour rating	Quality rating	Main event
	1. Alcohol 2. Food/bev. 3. Sports 4. Grooming 5. Autos 6. Other	1. Male 2. Female	(record actual number)	1. Not funny 2. 3. 4. 5. Very funny	1. Very low 2. 3. 4. 5. Very high	(write in your own words)
1	3	1	12	1	5	Boxing match

In the case of this illustration, the commercial advertised a 'sports' product, with a 'male' main character, including a dozen instances of violence, which was 'not funny', was of 'very high quality', and centred on a 'boxing match'.

You should note two things about this completed recording sheet. First, the commercial has now been coded, which means its features of interest (i.e., variables) have been translated into numbers (with the exception of the 'main event' variable, which we will deal with later). Second, the numbers in each cell represent the *coder's assessment* of the variable's attributes. The commercial did not report how humorous it was; the 'humour rating' came from the rater's own assessment.

Coding guidelines

If a 'rater' like you is expected to 'code' the properties of a commercial in a reliable manner, then you must have some coding guidelines. Coding guidelines give a rater some sense of what each variable refers to. Without a coding guideline, how would you know what 'main event' means?

Here are the coding guidelines you should follow in this pre-test lab. Each guideline refers to a variable and describes its meaning.

ID: This is an arbitrary identification number for each commercial to help keep the data organized.

Product type: Record the code number for the type of product being advertised. 'Alcohol' refers to any type of alcoholic beverage, and 'food/bev.' refers to restaurants and grocery chains, as well as any specific type of food or non-alcoholic beverage. 'Sports' includes anything related to amateur or professional sport, such as televised games and athletic clothing or footwear. 'Grooming' includes products like men's or women's cologne, shampoo, and shaving gear. 'Autos' refers to any type of motorized vehicle, including cars and trucks. Use the code 'other' for any product, service, or public service message that does not belong in the other five categories. In the case of 'other', write a one- or two-word description of the product beside or beneath the 'other' code.

Sex of main character: Does the commercial 'star' a male or a female? Record the code 1 for male and 2 for female. Often, a commercial will feature couples or groups of people, but you have to decide *which individual is the main character*. Only humans, including narrators, should be considered main characters, not animals or animated characters. Each commercial has a main character by virtue of that person's *prominent speaking or visual exposure*—i.e., the person is on the screen and/or is heard speaking for the longest period.

Instances of violence: Record the total number of times you see an instance of violence during the commercial.

Subjective humour rating: Rate the extent to which you find the commercial funny on a scale of 1 to 5, where 1 indicates 'not funny' and 5 indicates 'very funny'.

Subjective quality rating: Rate the quality of the commercial on a scale of 1 to 5, where 1 indicates 'very low' and 5 indicates 'very high'.

Main event: Describe in a few words what event is taking place in the commercial. Is it a party? A football game? Getting stopped by the police? Many things might occur, but try to choose the central one.

Two preliminary questions

You will recall that at the very least, coding requires (i) *good-quality variables* and (ii) *a reliable method* of assessment. The first requirement involves *mutually exclusive and exhaustive attributes*, while the second requirement involves good *operational definitions*. The data recording sheet and the coding guidelines are intended to meet these requirements.

Before you begin coding, your first task is to assess the information provided about each of the six variables in terms of these two requirements. In the space below, give your assessment of each of the six variables on these two accounts.

Variable: Product type

Are the attributes mutually exclusive? _____

Justification: _____

_____

Are the attributes exhaustive? _____

Justification: _____

_____

Is the operational definition sufficient to expect reliable coding? _____

Suggestions for improvement?

_____

_____

Variable: Sex of main character

Are the attributes mutually exclusive? _____

Justification: _____

_____

Are the attributes exhaustive? _____

Justification: _____

_____

Is the operational definition sufficient to expect reliable coding? _____

Suggestions for improvement?

_____

_____

Variable: Instances of violence

Are the attributes mutually exclusive? _____

Justification: _____

_____

Are the attributes exhaustive? _____

Justification: _____

_____

Is the operational definition sufficient to expect reliable coding? _____

Suggestions for improvement?

_____

_____

Variable: Humour rating

Are the attributes mutually exclusive? _____

Justification: _____

_____

Are the attributes exhaustive? _____

Justification: _____

_____

Is the operational definition sufficient to expect reliable coding? _____

Suggestions for improvement?

_____

_____

Variable: Quality rating

Are the attributes mutually exclusive? _____

Justification: _____

_____

Are the attributes exhaustive? _____

Justification: _____

_____

Is the operational definition sufficient to expect reliable coding? _____

Suggestions for improvement?

_____

_____

Variable: Main event

Are the attributes mutually exclusive? _____

Justification: _____

_____

Are the attributes exhaustive? _____

Justification: _____

_____

Is the operational definition sufficient to expect reliable coding? _____

Suggestions for improvement?

_____

_____

Trial coding

You are now familiar with the coding guidelines and the data recording sheet for the variables involved in this content analysis pre-test. So you are now in a position to put your knowledge to work and gain some experience with content analysis coding.

Your task is to view the small set of television commercials (Pre-test Commercials 1) linked to the companion website for this text (www.oupcanada.com/methodscoach) and code each one's content on the data recording sheet below.

For present purposes, use the coding scheme provided on the data recording sheet (even though you may have identified some deficiencies in the recording sheet during the previous exercise).

Table 7.3   Pre-test data recording sheet (Pre-test Commercials 1)

ID	Product type	Sex of main character	Instances of violence	Humour rating	Quality rating	Main event
	1. Alcohol 2. Food/bev. 3. Sports 4. Grooming 5. Autos 6. Other	1. Male 2. Female	(record actual number)	1. Not funny 2. 3. 4. 5. Very funny	1. Very low 2. 3. 4. 5. Very high	(write in your own words)
1						
2						
3						
4						

A reflection

Now you have had an introductory content analysis coding experience. On the basis of your experience, briefly answer the following questions:

How difficult was it to determine and code who the main character was in the various commercials?

What does this experience tell you about the importance of clear coding guidelines and their effect on data collection?

_____

_____

Improving the instrument

As mentioned previously, the coding guidelines are intended to give coders a sense of what each variable means and how it is to be measured in the content analysis. In research language, an ideal coding guideline would provide both a conceptual definition and an operational definition of the variable under consideration.

Look at the coding guideline for the variable 'instances of violence'. This guideline only provides an operational definition in that it specifies what to count for the variable.

To gain an appreciation of what goes into creating coding guidelines, take a closer look at the issue of violence in the commercials and elaborate on the definition in the space below.

Provide a conceptual definition of 'violence'.

_____

_____

Provide an alternate operational definition of 'violence' (in other words, create an operational definition that is different from the original one).

_____

_____

Additional coding

For more experience with coding and to test your alternate definition of 'violence', view the second set of commercials (Pre-test Commercials 2) linked to the companion website for this text (www.oupcanada.com/methodscoach), and complete the following recording sheet information.

Table 7.4   Pre-test data recording sheet (Pre-test Commercials 2)

ID	Product type	Sex of main character	Instances of violence	Humour rating	Quality rating	Main event
	1. Alcohol 2. Food/bev. 3. Sports 4. Grooming 5. Autos 6. Other	1. Male 2. Female	(record actual number)	1. Not funny 2. 3. 4. 5. Very funny	1. Very low 2. 3. 4. 5. Very high	(write in your own words)
5						
6						
7						
8						

Another reflection

The pre-testing phase of content analysis provides information that researchers can use to improve their data collection plan. It is not unusual for researchers to make changes based on the pre-testing experience.

Here is a conceptual definition of 'violence' that probably differs from the one you created: 'Violence is any deliberate act intended to cause physical harm to another person, regardless of whether or not they were in fact harmed.'

Specify the ways in which your conceptual definition differs from this one.

_____

_____

_____

If you were to use your alternate operational definition of violence to measure this new conceptual definition of violence, how well would you be measuring the concept under consideration?

_____

_____

_____

Imagine that 'violence' was to be operationalized as follows: Rate the level of violence on a 7-point scale, where 1 means 'no violence' and 7 means 'extreme violence'.

Would this operational definition be a better measure of the new conceptual definition of violence than yours? Justify your choice.

_____

_____

_____

Note: Remember to consult the 'Tips for lab applications' section on the companion website (www.oupcanada.com/methodscoach) if you find you need help.

LAB 8
Content Analysis: Collecting the Data

▌ Tune-up

The previous lab gave you some experience with pre-testing a coding scheme for a content analysis of television commercials. This lab extends the exercise and enables you to collect a reasonably large base of evidence that you can analyze.

In this lab, you will not draw on any new skill set. You will, however, be challenged to use skills developed in previous labs. Feel free to consult your earlier efforts when you address the questions posed in the lab.

LAB APPLICATION

Learning objectives

This lab assignment challenges you to clarify your understanding of:

- how variables are created for content analysis;
- the application of content analysis procedures.

Creating additional variables

Conducting a content analysis of the television commercials in fact involves scoring their properties on a variety of variables. In the previous lab, you pre-tested such an analysis using six variables.

Before coding a larger sample of commercials, let's expand the number of variables under consideration.

Below are three additional variables that could be coded in the commercials. For each variable, *create both a conceptual definition and an operational definition, as well as attributes for the variable.* Be sure to *draw on your pre-test experience* with the commercials to ensure that your definitions are *plausible.*

Variable 1: Age of main character

    Conceptual definition:

_____

_____

    Operational definition:

_____

_____

    Attributes:

_____

Variable 2: Race of main character

    Conceptual definition:

_____

_____

Operational definition:

_____

_____

Attributes:

_____

Variable 3: Status of main character

Conceptual definition:

_____

_____

Operational definition:

_____

_____

Attributes:

_____

Next, *double check the attributes* you have identified for each variable to ensure that they meet the criteria of mutual exclusiveness and exhaustiveness. If you identify any deficiencies on these accounts, make the appropriate corrections.

Updating the data recording sheet

At the end of this lab you will find a data recording sheet similar to the one used in the pre-testing exercise. Note, however, that the headings of the last three columns are blank. Use this space to record your scoring schemes for the three additional variables you have just created. Please *add the names and attributes of the three variables to the recording sheet.*

Gathering a content analysis data set

Now you are ready to gather content analysis evidence from a reasonably large sample of television commercials. For this exercise, use the coding guidelines provided in the pre-test, as well as the three new variables you have operationalized above.

Based on these fundamentals, you should now *view the file 'Television Commercials'* on the website associated with this text (www.oupcanada.com/methodscoach) and *complete a coding of each commercial* using the data recording sheet. Remember, your task is to identify a *single* score for *each* variable for *each* commercial.

Table 8.1 Television commercials data recording sheet

ID	Product type	Sex of main character	Instances of violence	Humour rating	Quality rating	Main event			
	1. Alcohol 2. Food/bev. 3. Sports 4. Grooming 5. Autos 6. Other	1. Male 2. Female	(record actual number)	1. Not funny 2. 3. 4. 5. Very funny	1. Very low 2. 3. 4. 5. Very high	(write in your own words)			

Note: Remember to consult the 'Tips for lab applications' section on the companion website (www.oupcanada.com/methodscoach) if you find you need help.

LAB 9
Content Analysis: Processing the Data

▶ Tune-up

In the previous two labs, you learned how to systematically collect content analysis evidence. Evidence is not collected for its own sake, however; it is collected for a purpose. The goal of this lab is to use the content analysis evidence you have collected to see what can be learned from it.

Summary analysis

Imagine that a research methods class containing 80 students completed writing a test. A week later, one of the students asks the professor, 'How did the class do on the test?' The professor responds by reciting 80 numbers, each of which represents one student's test score. It might sound like '76, 43, 92, 61, 57, 84, . . .' and so on until all 80 scores had been recited.

Although the professor actually answered the student's question, I think we can agree that the answer was not very helpful. The answer was not very helpful because it lacked one of the things we want from an analysis—*a summary*. Although the recitation of 80 test scores might be accurate, it is simply more information than an inquirer needs in order to get the point. What the questioner requires is a summary of how the class performed. This might take the form of the class average, for instance. Or it might be a table reporting how many students passed and how many failed.

All constructive analysis includes a summary, and the analysis of evidence from content analysis is no different in that regard. In its simplest form, a summary takes the evidence and reports *frequencies or percentages of occurrence*. Although simple, such tallies provide useful descriptive summaries of what the evidence reveals. We could, for instance, learn what percentage of the commercials were 'very funny'. Or we might find out what the average level of violence in the commercials was.

Of course, more sophisticated analyses of content analysis evidence can be conducted, including hypothesis testing. For now, however, you can learn a great deal from conducting and interpreting simple summaries.

Establishing reliability

In the previous labs, you gathered evidence about the variable properties of the television commercials. You did so by using the coding guidelines and making observations as carefully as you could. But for any number of reasons, your observations were probably imperfect. Perhaps the coding guidelines were vague or ambiguous; perhaps you forgot your glasses and couldn't see very well; perhaps the sound system was poor; perhaps thoughts of an impending term paper deadline distracted you—all quite understandable.

However understandable these imperfect observations might be, the practice of science requires identifying and mitigating these kinds of errors. One way of doing that is to examine the level of *reliability* in a set of observations. Reliability concerns the *consistency (repeatability)* of observations. To the extent that your coding of the commercials is similar to that of other coders, such coding consistency is probably *not due* to the idiosyncrasies of your situation. To the extent that the coding among different observers is inconsistent (i.e., unreliable), then skepticism about the quality of the observations arises.

In content analysis, the reliability of coding is calculated and interpreted through a measure called *inter-coder reliability* (sometimes called 'inter-rater reliability'). Inter-coder reliability literally involves *comparing the scores between two coders*. The greater the extent of agreement (consistency) between two coders' scores (i.e., observations), the higher the measurement's reliability. Note that inter-coder reliability can be calculated for *each variable*, since problems affecting the coding of one variable might not be present for another.

For any particular variable, the conventional way of calculating inter-coder reliability involves applying the following formula: *Number of cases with identical scores divided by total number of cases scored*. Think about what this calculation means. Say two coders scored 50 commercials on the variable 'level of pornography in the commercial'. If they disagreed on their rating for every commercial, the reliability would be zero (i.e., 0/50). If their scoring was the same on this variable for half the commercials, the reliability would be 0.50 (i.e., 25/50). And if they agreed on the scoring for every commercial on this variable, their coding would be perfectly reliable (i.e., 50/50 = 1.0).

The inter-rater reliability result tells you the *proportion* of cases in which coders scored a variable property the *same way*. A higher reliability rating for a particular variable indicates greater consistency in the coding of the variable. To assist you in interpreting the results, the following table should be helpful.

Table 9.1

Inter-rater reliability coefficient	Interpretation
0.90 or greater	Excellent
0.80–0.89	Very good
0.70–0.79	Satisfactory
0.60–0.69	Marginal
Less than 0.60	Poor

This table lets you translate the results of a particular coefficient into evaluative language. For instance, an inter-rater reliability coefficient of 0.73 for the variable 'level of pornography' would be interpreted as following: *There is satisfactory reliability in the coding of the variable 'level of pornography' among the commercials.*

Open-ended coding

The summary analysis and inter-rater reliability assessments are useful techniques for content analysis variables that have used 'closed-ended coding'. Closed-ended coding applies to variables whose *attributes* have been specified *in advance*. When you simply record digits in the cells of the data recording sheet, you are employing closed-ended codes. The digits you record are your selections among the *pre-existing* set of mutually exclusive and exhaustive codes.

Not all variables have pre-established codes. Sometimes coding involves *jotting down notes* about what was observed concerning the variable of interest. In the last lab you did this, for instance, with the variable 'main event'. Such coding is called 'open-ended' because you are free (i.e., 'open') to make whatever notes you like regarding your observations.

Analyzing content analysis variables that have used open-ended codes calls for an additional step before using summarization or reliability assessment techniques. This step requires *transforming your coding notes into a set of mutually exclusive and exhaustive categories*. In other words, this step requires you to create a good-quality variable.

Creating and conducting the coding of open-ended variables is somewhat of an art. However, the following set of steps should make the task easier:

1. Read through the open-ended notes and comments you wrote for the variable under consideration.
2. As you are reading, try to imagine what 'label' you would give each comment (i.e., what 'type' of response it is).
3. See if you can create four or five 'types' (labels) that will capture all of the open-ended responses. These 'types' will become the *new attributes* for the variable.
4. After you have created the types (attributes), check them to see that they meet the mutually exclusive and exhaustive criteria.
5. If possible, arrange the attributes in some kind of order.
6. Assign each of the new attributes a number (code).

After completing this exercise, you will have transformed the open-ended codes into a closed-ended scheme. However, this closed-ended scheme is not pre-determined and imposed on the evidence. Instead, the new coding scheme will be inductively generated and customized to suit the idiosyncrasies of the observations you noted.

With this transformation in place, your final task is to apply the new coding scheme to your open-ended comments. This is really an exercise in *re-coding*, and it is very similar to the original closed-ended coding you have done. In this case, however, you are *not* applying the coding scheme to the commercials themselves. Instead you are applying the new coding scheme to the *notes and comments* you made about the commercials.

To check the adequacy of your coding scheme, you can conduct a couple of checks. First, you should check that applying the codes to your notes has resulted in (i) separate comments each only being assigned a single code (assuring mutual exclusiveness) and (ii) all comments having a code assigned (assuring exhaustiveness). This is a critical test, and if you detect inadequacy on either account, the coding scheme must be reworked and reapplied. The second check is to calculate the inter-rater reliability coefficient.

LAB 9 APPLICATION

Learning objectives

The following lab questions are directed at helping you translate the tune-up points into concrete research situations. Specifically, this lab assignment challenges you to clarify your understanding of:

- how content analysis evidence is summarized;
- how inter-rater reliability codes are calculated and interpreted;
- how open-ended coding is managed.

Note: This application uses the evidence you gathered and reported on the data recording sheet in the previous lab.

Summarizing evidence

The cells of your data recording sheet contain numbers as well as some notes and comments. To make sense of this evidence, you must summarize it. The following questions regarding each of the variables will give you practice.

1. Product type

    Which product type was most common in the commercials?

    _____

    What percentage of the commercials included this product type?

    _____%

2. Sex of main character

    What percentage of the commercials starred a male? _____%

3. Instances of violence

    What percentage of commercials contained at least one instance of violence? _____%

4. Humour

    What percentage had ratings above 3 (i.e., above average)? _____%

5. Quality

    What percentage had ratings above 3 (i.e., above average)? _____%

Establishing coding reliability

Establishing reliability requires a comparison of the *consistency* between *different* codings of the same evidence. Your data recording sheet only includes a single coding of the evidence (i.e., yours). Therefore, to calculate the inter-coder reliability, you need another coding of the evidence. You will find an additional data recording sheet with a second set of codes on the website for this book (www.oupcanada.com/methodscoach). It is much like the form below, except that there are numbers in the columns identified as '2nd code' for each variable.

Table 9.2

ID	Product type Your code	Product type 2nd code	Sex Your code	Sex 2nd code	Violence Your code	Violence 2nd code	Humour Your code	Humour 2nd code	Quality Your code	Quality 2nd code
1										
2										
3										
4										
5										
6										
7										
8										
9										
10										
11										
12										
13										
14										
15										
16										
17										
18										
19										
20										

Steps in determining inter-coder reliability

1. Transfer the appropriate data from the '2nd code' column of the website data onto your data recording sheet.

2. For *each variable*, count the number of commercials on which there was *coding agreement*. Record this number in the 'numerator' column of the table following these steps. As an example, the circled cases below indicate what 'coding agreement' means.

Table 9.3

ID	Product type		Sex		Violence		Humour		Quality	
	You	2nd	You	2nd	You	2nd	You	2nd	You	2nd
E.g.	1	1	2	2	0	2	3	4	4	4

3. For *each variable*, count the total number of commercials that were coded. Record this number in the 'denominator' column of the table following these steps. Note that the denominator result should be the same for each variable.

4. Calculate the inter-coder reliability coefficient for *each variable*. Record the coefficient in the third column of the table below. Note that the coefficient is calculated as follows:

$$\frac{\text{Number of cases with identical values}}{\text{Total number of cases coded.}}$$

5. Interpret each of the coefficients you have calculated, using the table provided in the tune-up sections (Table 9.1). Record your interpretation in the final column of the table.

Table 9.4

VARIABLE	Numerator	Denominator	Coefficient	Interpretation
Product type				
Sex of main character				
Number of violent instances				
Subjective humour rating				
Subjective quality rating				

Review the inter-coder reliability coefficients, and select the variable with the *highest* coefficient and the variable with the *lowest* coefficient.

Based on your experience with coding the variables, identify the *reasons* that might explain why one of these variables is coded more reliably than the other.

_____

_____

_____

_____

_____

Note: Remember to consult the 'Tips for lab applications' section on the companion website (www.oupcanada.com/methodscoach) if you find you need help.

LAB 10
Qualitative Field Observation

▶ Tune-up

Unobtrusive measures

There is much to be learned from the direct observation and direct questioning of people. But such methods have their own problems, many of which centre on the fact that *knowing that they are being observed often changes people*. In physical science, this phenomenon is known as the 'Heisenberg uncertainty principle'; in the social sciences, it is referred to as the 'Hawthorne effect'. But anyone who has pointed a camera in someone's direction and has seen how they change (by changing their facial expression, 'fixing' their hair, and so on) has a sense of the effect.

One way of avoiding such distortions of 'subject reaction' is to use unobtrusive measures. Unobtrusive measures are methods of collecting evidence without the knowledge of the subject. Because the subjects are unaware of the data collection, they are not in a position to react to it, and their 'non-reaction' prevents the potential distortion.

Unobtrusive measures are generally classified into two types, covert and indirect. Covert measures are carried out without the explicit awareness and consent of the people or group being observed. Secretly taking notes, using one-way mirrors, or attending meetings under the pretext of being a group member are examples of covert measures. Although many classic studies have been conducted using covert measures (e.g., Laud Humphreys's *Tearoom Trade*; Leon Festinger and his colleagues' *When Prophecy Fails*), these techniques have fallen out of favour in recent decades because of the serious ethical issues they raise (e.g., the obligation to obtain informed consent).

However, indirect unobtrusive measures do not present such ethical challenges, since they focus on what persons or groups have 'left behind'. Indirect measures utilize the 'traces' or residuals of human action. One conventional distinction of the evidence that persons 'leave behind' is to distinguish between 'erosion' and 'accretion' measures.

Erosion measures refer to those in which the activities of people have left trace evidence in the form of *deterioration*—the evidence has been 'ground away' (eroded). For example, an erosion measure of the popularity of an art exhibit might be the degree of wear and tear on the floor tiles surrounding the exhibit. The more popular an exhibit, the greater the erosion of the floor tiles.

Accretion measures, on the other hand, consist of trace evidence that has *accumulated* because of people's activities. For example, the attractiveness of various types of fish in an aquarium or pet store might be measured by the amount of smudging on the glass as a result of people tapping on the fish tanks. In another classic illustration, the popularity of radio stations in a city was measured by checking vehicles left for repair at service stations and determining what station their radios were tuned to.

Qualitative coding

The act of coding involves the classification or 'grouping' of evidence into coherent categories. The resulting groups identify 'types'. For example, Émile Durkheim identified four classic types of suicide, including egoistic, altruistic, anomic, and fatalistic. His classification is useful in distinguishing between and sorting suicides in terms of their connection to participants' levels of social integration and regulation.

Commonly, coding is an activity performed *using pre-existing categories*. In other words, the codes and their respective meanings already exist, and the researcher's task is to assign the codes appropriately. So with respect to the variable 'sex', for example, the researcher assigns a '1' to males and a '2' to females. This is largely what coding in quantitative analysis involves.

Qualitative data collection and analysis requires a different approach because the data are more open and amorphous. Consequently, the coding project is not a matter of assigning pre-existing codes but of finding 'meaning' in the evidence. In this respect, the coding exercise for qualitative data is more inductive than deductive.

To a considerable extent, the inductive process involved in qualitative coding is an art. Labelling the process an art is intended to suggest that it is not one guided by well-defined steps but instead requires a more creative approach. Even so, the following tips should help you with the process.

1. Appreciate that the 'content' of what you are coding are specific 'cases', and it is your task to identify the general conceptual 'category' (rather like the television program *Jeopardy*: the specific qualitative content is the 'answer', and identifying the general conceptual category means specifying the correct 'question').
2. Identifying general conceptual categories requires *defining* meaningful labels. The process is not a matter of discovering pre-existing categories; rather, it is a matter of *declaration*. In other words, *you* decide and justify the 'types' in the classification scheme.
3. The goal of your classification scheme is to 'make sense' of the qualitative evidence. In this case, 'sense' is 'made' by identifying the *general* case that is illustrated by the *specific* instance.
4. A basic way of identifying general categories is to look for different *themes* around which the evidence can be organized. Each distinctive theme is then defined by a different *label*. These labels, in turn, become the names of the coding categories.
5. When looking for themes, it is worth noting the distinction between *manifest content* and *latent content*. This distinction points to just what the labels say—namely, that the way something appears on the surface (i.e., manifest) is not necessarily the whole story. Therefore, you should look to see whether there is an underlying (i.e., latent) meaning to the content. By keeping this distinction in mind, you will learn to attend not just to the 'literal' meaning of things but to their 'symbolic' importance as well.

LAB 10 APPLICATION

Learning objectives

The following lab questions are directed at helping you translate the tune-up points into concrete research situations. Specifically, this lab assignment challenges you to clarify your understanding of:

- collecting and interpreting accretion measures;
- collecting and interpreting erosion measures.

Graffiti analysis

Graffiti dates back at least to ancient Greek and Roman civilizations. Evidence indicates that Roman citizens wrote vulgar passages, criticisms of political leaders, sexual innuendo, advertisements for prostitution, declarations of love, and other epithets on places such as the walls of public baths and toilets and on monuments.

In modern urban environments, graffiti is pervasive. We can view its content as unobtrusive measures of the 'accretion' type. Much of the graffiti seen in urban settings is incomprehensible (but often quite attractive) to outsiders, since it centres on the 'tagging' artwork done by members of specific subcultures. The following example is of this type:

Figure 10.1 Graffiti

However, there is still a great deal of 'old-fashioned' graffiti around—the type involving an individual writing or scratching a message on a wall or pillar, using (more or less) standard vocabulary.

In this exercise, your first task is to try your hand at developing some thematic codes for pre-recorded graffiti.

Pre-recorded graffiti

Below is a list of 19 instances of graffiti gathered from outside the library at a local university. Several statements that seem to share the same theme have been identified and are linked to boxes A, B, or C.

Examine and analyze the graffiti items that are grouped together. For each box, *identify what you think is a plausible theme* that connects the shared items. *Justify* your choices.

Box A

    Theme: _____

    Justification: _____

    _____

    _____

Box B

    Theme: _____

    Justification: _____

    _____

    _____

Box C

    Theme: _____

    Justification: _____

    _____

    _____

Verbatim Graffiti Statements

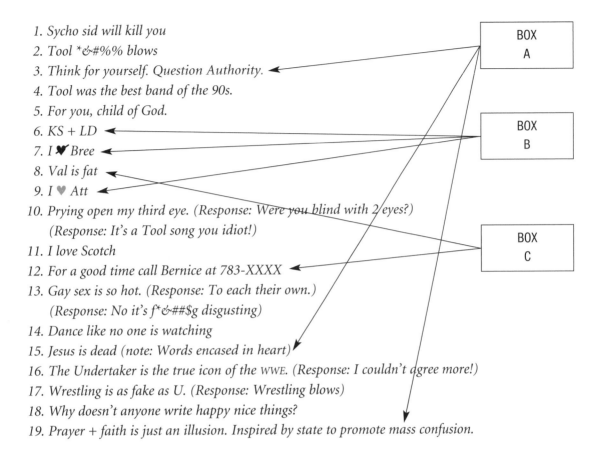

1. *Sycho sid will kill you*
2. *Tool *&#%% blows*
3. *Think for yourself. Question Authority.*
4. *Tool was the best band of the 90s.*
5. *For you, child of God.*
6. *KS + LD*
7. *I ♥ Bree*
8. *Val is fat*
9. *I ♥ Att*
10. *Prying open my third eye. (Response: Were you blind with 2 eyes?)*
    (Response: It's a Tool song you idiot!)
11. *I love Scotch*
12. *For a good time call Bernice at 783-XXXX*
13. *Gay sex is so hot. (Response: To each their own.)*
    (Response: No it's f&##$g disgusting)*
14. *Dance like no one is watching*
15. *Jesus is dead (note: Words encased in heart)*
16. *The Undertaker is the true icon of the WWE. (Response: I couldn't agree more!)*
17. *Wrestling is as fake as U. (Response: Wrestling blows)*
18. *Why doesn't anyone write happy nice things?*
19. *Prayer + faith is just an illusion. Inspired by state to promote mass confusion.*

BOX A

BOX B

BOX C

Collecting graffiti

Now that you have a sense of how graffiti can be qualitatively analyzed, you can try your hand at extending the technique, following the instructions below.

1. *Locate a spot*, such as a bathroom stall or study carrel on campus or at any other location where you are likely to find graffiti.
2. In the space provided below, *record the various instances of graffiti* that you find. Try to fill a complete page with examples. Make sure that you (i) focus on written words rather than on drawings or art, (ii) try to record things written on a single wall or other surface, and (iii) try to record as many different writers as you can. Make sure that you write the words verbatim (i.e., exactly as written).
3. *Conduct an open coding* of your data and *justify* your results.

In what location did you record the graffiti? (Be specific.)

In the spaces below, record the instances of graffiti.

1. _____
2. _____
3. _____
4. _____
5. _____
6. _____
7. _____
8. _____
9. _____
10. _____
11. _____
12. _____
13. _____
14. _____
15. _____
16. _____
17. _____
18. _____
19. _____
20. _____
21. _____
22. _____
23. _____
24. _____
25. _____

Identify the *themes* in your evidence.

Theme 1: _____

Record the numbers of the items that relate to this theme.

_____

Provide a justification explaining how the contents of the specific items are connected to the shared theme.

_____

_____

_____

_____

Theme 2: _____

Record the numbers of the items that relate to this theme.

_____

Provide a justification explaining how the contents of the specific items are connected to the shared theme.

_____

_____

_____

_____

Theme 3: _____

Record the numbers of the items that relate to this theme.

_____

Provide a justification explaining how the contents of the specific items are connected to the shared theme.

_____

_____

_____

_____

Theme 4: _____

    Record the numbers of the items that relate to this theme.

    _____

    Provide a justification explaining how the contents of the specific items are connected to the shared theme.

    _____

    _____

    _____

    _____

Theme 5: _____

    Record the numbers of the items that relate to this theme.

    _____

    Provide a justification explaining how the contents of the specific items are connected to the shared theme.

    _____

    _____

    _____

    _____

Unanticipated travel routes

The landscape architects who plan public spaces commonly make accommodation for people to move through the space. They typically do so by providing sidewalks. Quite often, however, people prefer to use travel routes of their own making. These 'new' routes are known as 'unanticipated travel routes' (UTRs).

UTRs are typically 'erosion' measures, since their use involves the 'wearing away' of the existing landscape—which is why landscape architects abhor UTRs!

Below is a map identifying the location of several UTRs at one university campus location. Study the location of the identified routes.

Figure 10.2 UTR map

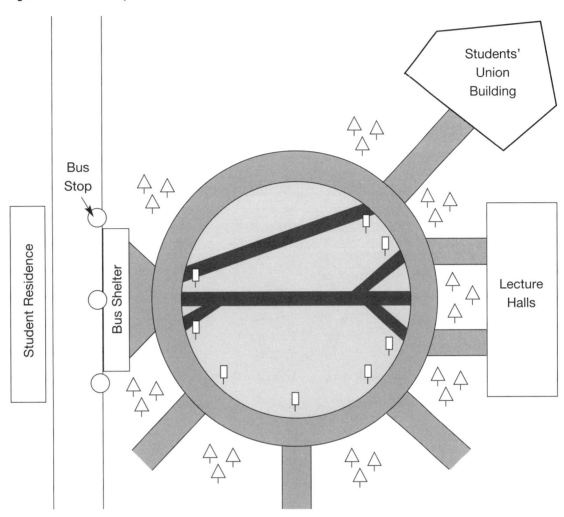

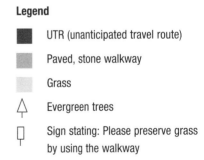

Legend

■ UTR (unanticipated travel route)

▨ Paved, stone walkway

▢ Grass

△ Evergreen trees

⬚ Sign stating: Please preserve grass by using the walkway

From the information provided, what would you say is the principal reason for participants using these routes?

_____

What does this reason tell you about the users' priorities? How do these priorities compare to the presumed priorities of the landscape architect who designed the space?

Users' priorities: _____

Landscape architect's priorities: _____

Now that you have a sense of how such 'erosion' UTRs can be analyzed, you can try your hand at extending this technique to your local situation.

Local UTRs

1. Identify one or more *familiar location(s)* on your campus or in your neighbourhood where UTRs are evident. Identify *at least three* UTRs.
2. *Draw a map of the location(s)*, identifying where the UTRs are relative to various relevant landmarks (e.g., bus stops, parking lots, convenience stores, lecture halls).
3. *Spend at least 10 minutes observing the conduct* of people using the UTRs. Record your observations.
4. Based on your observations, develop a justification for *each* UTR, explaining why it exists where it does.
5. From your separate explanations, develop some *general conclusions* about the *concerns of people who walk*.
6. Your conclusions are based solely on your observations. Identify and justify *some other method* you could use to confirm the validity of your conclusions.

UTR 1

Observations of users:

_____

_____

_____

Explanation of UTR existence:

_____

_____

_____

UTR 2

Observations of users:

_____

_____

_____

Explanation of UTR existence:

_____

_____

_____

UTR 3

Observations of users:

_____

_____

_____

Explanation of UTR existence:

_____

_____

_____

Inductive general conclusions about concerns of walkers:

_____

_____

_____

Justification of alternate method for confirming general conclusions:

_____

_____

_____

_____

Note: Remember to consult the 'Tips for lab applications' section on the companion website (www.oupcanada.com/methodscoach) if you find you need help.

LAB 11
Using Existing and Official Statistics

▶ Tune-up

Social construction of evidence

The average citizen has little knowledge of the process of scientific activity. Casual questioning reveals that a common stereotype of 'scientists' and their activity is modelled on the Mr Spock character in the *Star Trek* television series—intelligent, cool, calculating, and value-free. In the public mind, scientists are quite 'alien' in the sense that they can perform feats quite foreign to the average person, such as suspending their values or taking an objective reading of a situation.

At the very least, your study of research methods should debunk this stereotype. Scientific activity is performed by ordinary, interested people who have some specialized training related to the theory and methods of their discipline. Stated differently, science is really a 'cultural script' that actors follow (more or less), which results in socially constructed products. In this sense, it is similar to all 'games' that people play.

Power of science

Science is one cultural script that humans have developed over the ages to reduce uncertainty and increase knowledge. But it is only one among many. Common sense, tradition, meditation, revelation, and authority (to name a few) are also methods that humans continue to use to increase their understanding of how the world works.

In the modern world, however, scientific knowing has a more prominent place than many of these other methods. There are many reasons for the prominence of science, but it is largely because science has become institutionalized in modern societies. Such institutionalization involves a cultural commitment to scientific beliefs, norms, and values and an enormous number of organizations and actors, consuming large quantities of all forms of capital, to produce scientific results across a range of fields.

Institutionalization enhances the presence and power of science relative to other ways of knowing. Such power legitimizes science and its products. Imagine your physician telling you that he or she had a 'revelation' that you had lung cancer. You would probably consider the claim absurd. Note how different your reaction would be if you were told that 'scientific tests' revealed that you had cancer. Both are claims, but the perceived legitimacy of the method makes a tremendous difference in their relative power.

Assertion versus demonstration

The cultural legitimacy and power of scientific claims has a downside. The institutional weight and inertia of science makes it easy (sometime too easy) to accept assertions that are declared to be 'scientific'. The tendency is to believe scientific assertions as though they came from some independent, infallible source of 'truth'—which of course they do not. Naive acceptance of any claims (no matter what the source) is risky.

Minimizing the risk centres on placing a higher priority on 'demonstration' than on 'assertion'. In methodological terms, this involves repeatedly responding to any claim (assertion) with the question 'How do you know?' This question inquires about the nature of the reasoning and evidence supporting a conclusion.

Official and unofficial statistics

Among the many benefits of rising computer and Internet use is the availability of results from ongoing research. When these results derive from national or large-scale government research (often survey research), they are referred to as 'official statistics'. Note that the designation 'official' gives these government reports and publications an air of importance that promotes their acceptance.

In addition to this empirical evidence, there is another kind of evidence that can be considered 'official'. This evidence comes from findings that appear in peer-reviewed scientific journals. These results are official in the sense that they have passed a rigorous review process conducted by informed experts.

Both types of official statistics have an aura of legitimacy because both the process and the product of the research are public. In other words, interested observers can examine how the study was conducted to see what imperfections it might have. The possibility of public scrutiny does not make the results infallible, but it does make their flaws more apparent—which is a vitally important consideration.

In contrast to official statistics, the processes of many kinds of research products are not made public. These products may be considered 'unofficial' in that their research processes are undocumented or their findings have not undergone expert review before they are reported.

Whether official or unofficial, statistical results need to be understood not as declared 'truth' but as socially constructed products. To be properly appreciated, they must be subjected to the 'how do you know?' question. The answer to this question will lead you to a consideration of the many methodological issues you are being exposed to in your research methods course. Applying the tools you have acquired to the quality of variables, the nature of reasoning, and the need for clear conceptual and operational definitions, as well as the strengths and weaknesses of various data collection strategies, will take you a long way toward understanding the credibility or incredibility of many official and unofficial claims.

LAB 11 APPLICATION

Learning objectives

The following lab questions are directed at helping you translate the tune-up points into concrete research situations. Specifically, this lab assignment challenges you to clarify your understanding of:

■ estimating the credibility of unofficial statistics using official statistics.

The misuse of official statistics

Social issues and evidence

Canadian society is comprised of a network of interconnected institutions and organizations that serve a variety of collective purposes. Like all societies, ours is imperfect at serving the needs of its citizens. There is always room for critical observation, assessment, and improvement.

One way the public becomes aware of social issues that need remedial attention is through the steady stream of reports appearing in the mass media. Many of these reports use unofficial statistics to justify the nature of the social need.

This application focuses on one illustration of a social issue in the news that relies on unofficial statistics as part of its justification.

The scale and scope of eating disorders

The following newspaper report briefly outlines the scope of the eating disorders issue in Manitoba:

> The statistics are shocking. According to the National Eating Disorder Information Centre, 11,000 women in Manitoba currently suffer from eating disorders. For females between 15 and 24 years old, the annual death rate from anorexia is more than 12 times higher than the death rate from all other causes combined. (*Winnipeg Free Press* 17 September 2002, p. D1)

Regarding the situation in Canada as a whole, *Time* magazine (18 July 2005, p. 37) cited a commonly reported estimate in an article on 'pro-anorexia websites':

> Nobody knows for certain how many of the estimated 11 million Americans, 1 million Canadians, and 200,000 Australians suffering from anorexia or bulimia visit those websites.

These examples typify the kind of reporting about social concerns that can be found in newspapers and on radio and television broadcasts. Its basic form is to highlight and justify the need to address a social issue by reference to official statistics.

However, it is always worthwhile to cast a critical eye on the evidence used to justify claims. The following exercise will take you through a critical assessment exercise and persuade you that, with only a little effort, you can obtain an independent sense of a claim's legitimacy.

The health field makes an important distinction between the concepts of 'morbidity' and 'mortality'. Mortality refers to death, while morbidity refers to illness. It is common to distinguish statistics in terms of which of these components of ill health is the referent. This exercise looks at the issue of eating disorders in terms of mortality and morbidity in turn.

1. Mortality

For the moment, let's assume that the newspaper report is accurate. Using the statistics in the report, *make a rough guess about the number of anorexia nervosa deaths you would expect to see in a given year among young women (aged 15–24) in Canada and in Manitoba.* Report your estimates below. (Note: Anorexia nervosa is usually considered one of several types of eating disorder, including bulimia nervosa.)

Canada: In Canada, the population of females aged 15–24 at the time of the newspaper report was about 1,980,000. Estimated number of deaths from anorexia nervosa =

_____

Manitoba: In Manitoba, the population of females aged 15–24 at the time of the newspaper report was about 77,900. Estimated number of deaths from anorexia nervosa =

_____

Statistics Canada's *Vital Statistics Compendium* contains official data on the *actual number of deaths* in Canada by age, sex, and province, and as a result of specific causes, as well as standardized *death rates* (i.e., number of deaths, taking into account population size, which indicates the risk of death in a given year).

Let's use some existing statistics from the *Vital Statistics Compendium* to gauge the accuracy of the newspaper report and then your estimate based on it. Below are two pieces of information from the compendium.[1] The first is a table of the 'Leading causes of death by age (15–24 years) and sex'. The second is a conceptual definition of what Statistics Canada means by the concept 'leading causes of death'.

Table 11.1 Leading causes of death by age (15–24 years) and sex, Canada

Cause	MALES		FEMALES	
	Deaths	Percent	Deaths	Percent
Unintentional injuries	801	45.4	267	41.9
Suicide	490	27.8	91	14.3
Cancer	98	5.6	56	8.8
Heart diseases	35	2.0	18	2.8
Congenital anomalies	26	1.5	15	2.4
HIV infection	12	0.7	4	0.6
Cerebrovascular diseases	10	0.6	5	0.8
Other causes	292	16.6	181	28.4
Total	**1,764**	**100.0**	**637**	**100.0**

Source: Adapted from Statistics Canada, *Vital Statistics Compendium*, Catalogue no. 84-214-XPE.

Leading causes of death—refers to the main causes of death in terms of frequency of occurrence, using meaningful aggregations of specific causes. (An example of a meaningful aggregation is 'death due to heart diseases', which comprises a number of different conditions, such as acute myocardial infarction and cardiomyopathy.) A specific cause of death is not aggregated with others if the number of deaths attributed to that cause is particularly high, or its importance as a morbid condition warrants a ranking of its own (e.g., suicide, HIV infection).

Carefully read the conceptual definition of 'leading causes of death' used by Statistics Canada. Using this definition, examine the evidence in the table on leading causes of death.

With this evidence in mind, reread the newspaper report on eating disorders. *What part of the report does the vital statistics evidence put into question? Justify your claim.*

Problematic claim in the newspaper report:

_____

_____

Justification: _____

_____

_____

_____

_____

The following table reproduces the *females'* leading causes of death information for Canada. The table also includes a column that converts the percentage of deaths from various causes into *proportions*. Above this information is the estimated death rate for 15- to 24-year-old females in Canada and Manitoba.

Using the information in the table, *calculate* and *record* the 'estimated number' of deaths among 15- to 24-year-old females in Manitoba from various causes.

Table 11.2 Mortality among females aged 15–24, for Canada and Manitoba

	Canada		Manitoba
Total number of deaths (all causes)	637		17
Death rate (deaths per 1,000 females aged 15–24)	0.3		0.2–0.3
Leading causes of death	Number	Proportion	Estimated number
Accidents	267	0.419	
Suicides	91	0.143	
Cancer	56	0.088	
Heart disease	18	0.028	
Birth defects	15	0.024	
HIV	4	0.006	
Stroke	5	0.008	
Other causes	181	0.284	
Total (all causes)	**637**	**1.000**	

Based on the 15- to 24-year-old female deaths reported in the table, what is the *maximum possible numbers of deaths from anorexia nervosa in Canada and Manitoba*? Record your answer below.

Canada: _____

Manitoba: _____

Justify your estimates of the maximum anorexia nervosa deaths.

_____

_____

_____

_____

_____

2. Morbidity

According to recent peer-reviewed medical research published by Hoek (2006),[2] 'the average prevalence rates for anorexia nervosa and bulimia nervosa among young females are 0.3% and 1.0% respectively.' If these research-based estimates are accurate, what is the number of females aged 15 to 24 we can expect to be suffering from these diseases in Canada and Manitoba? (Use the population figures provided earlier to calculate your estimate.)

Canada: Anorexia nervosa estimate _____

               Bulimia estimate _____

               Combined estimate _____

Manitoba: Anorexia nervosa estimate _____

               Bulimia estimate _____

               Combined estimate _____

Compare your estimates with the figures reported in the newspaper and *Time* magazine quotations provided earlier. If we assume that the prevalence rates given by Hoek are correct, what do your estimates suggest about the accuracy of the estimates in these mass media reports?

_____

_____

_____

_____

_____

_____

_____

_____

Note: Remember to consult the 'Tips for lab applications' section on the companion website (www.oupcanada.com/methodscoach) if you find you need help.

LAB 12
Causal Thinking

▶ Tune-up

Scientific 'understanding'

Contrary to popular belief, experience is not a very good teacher. Recall your experience of a beautiful sunrise or sunset. Your eyes took in the majestic beauty of it all, but what does this experience teach you? How do your observations help you to understand the beauty generated by the rising or setting sun? In fact, your direct experience of this (or any) phenomenon teaches you very little.

The learning that enhances your understanding requires you to *interpret* your experience. Interpretation can take various forms, but in general, it involves appreciating how your particular experience is connected to some general case. When you 'understand' something about a sunrise or sunset, for example, you comprehend it in terms of the earth's rotation on its axis, angle of inclination, and atmospheric refraction.

In terms of science, understanding of experience is enhanced through the identification of 'causes' and 'effects'. Establishing these linkages enables us to understand how the experienced event fits into a general chain of events.

The importance of causes

For researchers, 'causes' refer to the 'real' (actual) reasons why some event occurred. Causes are not to be confused with 'justifications', which are *plausible* reasons for an event's occurrence.

Researchers place a great deal of importance on identifying causes, because causes play a pivotal role in two key scientific activities—explanation and prediction. *Explanation* is a historical activity and refers to understanding events that have occurred in the past. *Prediction*, by contrast, is a future-oriented activity and involves anticipating upcoming events. Explanation and prediction are really flip sides of the same thing—causal identification. To adequately understand why some event occurred (i.e., explain it) requires the identification of causes: The woman kicked the door *because* she was frustrated. In a parallel way, identifying the existence of an operating cause allows one to anticipate (predict) an outcome: Observing that the woman is frustrated, you predict that she will kick the door.

Conventional causal criteria

Sorting out which independent variable is the actual 'cause' of change in some dependent variable is a matter of demonstration—not declaration. Someone stating that two variables are causally linked does not make the case. The status of variables as identified 'causes' needs to be demonstrated.

Causal demonstration typically involves ensuring that three tests are 'passed'. The first test is to demonstrate that there is an actual relationship between the variables under consideration. You will recall (from Lab 1) that the sign of a relationship is that a change in one variable is systematically related to change in another variable. Passing this first test satisfies the causal criterion of 'association' (correlation). The second causal test is to demonstrate that the association apparent in the first test is a genuine (authentic) connection. You will recall (from Lab 2) that appearances can fool the observer. On closer inspection, not all apparent relationships are 'real'. Demonstrating that the relationship between independent and dependent variables is genuine satisfies the second causal criterion, that of 'non-spuriousness'. The third causal test is the test of 'sequence'. This test requires that the time-ordering of the variables be demonstrated in a manner that shows the independent variable changed *prior to* changes in the dependent variable. In short, researchers must provide evidence of appropriately sequenced, non-spurious associations between the independent and dependent variables before asserting that changing one variable 'causes' change in another variable.

Additional criteria

Sequence, association, and non-spuriousness are the standard criteria that researchers use to demonstrate 'causation'. In addition to these three tests, some researchers include two additional criteria—'necessity' and 'sufficiency'. 'Necessity' means that a particular condition *must be* present in order for the observed effect to occur. For example, the consumption of alcohol is a necessary condition in a charge of 'drunk driving'. Likewise, it is necessary for air temperature to be below zero degrees Celsius for ice to form. The criterion of 'sufficiency' is different. The sufficiency criterion states that a condition is enough to produce the change in the outcome variable. Making an obscene remark to a professor is sufficient to have you barred from class. Drinking a large bottle of water is sufficient to quench your thirst.

Internal and external validity

The aphorism that 'everything costs something' is no less true in research than in other areas of life. The quest to meet the criteria needed to establish causation generally requires researchers to tighten their control. As researchers become more confident that they can attribute dependent variable outcomes to changes in the independent variable rather than to flaws in the research design, they refer to the investigation having 'internal validity'.

Research designs with the most control are 'experimental', and to evaluate the quality of various experimental designs, researchers look at a variety of common 'threats' to internal validity. These threats include:

- *History*: Conducting research studies takes time. It is possible that during the time period (history) when the study is occurring, changes other than those of the independent variable occur. If this happens, it becomes difficult to isolate the specific effects of the independent variable.
- *Maturation*: During the time a research study is being conducted, the subjects can change, either biologically or psychologically (maturation). When these changes occur, isolating the effects of the independent variable becomes more challenging.
- *Selection*: A group receiving some intervention (i.e., the independent variable) is 'experimental' and needs to be compared to another group ('control') that does not receive the intervention. If these experimental and control groups are not equivalent at the outset (selection), then attributing differences identified later becomes problematic.
- *Testing*: Researchers are interested in identifying the effects of an independent variable on a dependent variable. However, measuring the dependent variable requires testing. It is possible that the act of testing (measuring) the dependent variable creates its own effects.
- *Instrumentation*: Changes in the dependent variable do not always signify actual changes in the subjects being measured. Sometimes differences in observed outcomes can be due to changes in the measuring instruments.
- *Regression*: When groups are selected because they have an extreme value on a dependent variable (e.g., extremely prejudiced), the most likely trend for them to follow is to move toward the average—no matter what intervention occurs. This can be an important confounding factor that disguises the genuine effects of the intervention.
- *Mortality*: When subjects drop out of an experiment for any reason, their absence is likely to bias the equivalence between the comparison groups. Therefore, when the groups are compared in the final analysis, differences may be due to differing group composition rather than to independent variable effects.

High-quality experimental designs avoid or minimize these sources of invalidity and in doing so allow a clearer interpretation of the causal impact an independent variable has on a dependent variable. However, achieving sufficient control to keep these sources of contamination in check usually comes at a cost—a cost to the external validity of the research.

External validity refers to whether the findings of the study are generalizable in the 'real world'. As a general rule, as the internal validity of a study is enhanced, the study becomes more 'artificial' and therefore loses some external validity. Think of the introductory psychology students who participate in experiments as part of their course credit. How typical of everyday Canadians are first-year university students? How typical of real-world conditions are the experimental situations they find themselves in?

LAB 12 APPLICATION

Learning objectives

The following lab questions are directed at helping you translate the tune-up points into concrete research situations. Specifically, this lab assignment challenges you to clarify your understanding of:

- confusing causes and justifications;
- how experiments handle causal criteria;
- how natural experiments distinguish causes;
- the difference between necessity and sufficiency;
- internal and external validity.

Causes and justifications

It is a near certainty that when a university exam is held at a particular time on a certain date, some students will not show up to write. Later on, these students usually appear in the professor's office to explain their absence. In this situation, it is common for the professor to ask, 'Why didn't you show up for the exam?' Here are some actual explanations that students have offered in recent years:

- 'My grandmother died.'
- 'I was lonely and desperate, so I left the country for a few days.'
- 'My car wouldn't start, and I couldn't find money for bus fare.'
- 'While driving to the exam, I became very sick and vomited all over my clothes.'
- 'I hadn't completed my studying and was unprepared to write.'
- 'My snake ate my pet rat, and I was so traumatized that I couldn't come to the exam.'

In the space below, explain how these 'reasons' for missing an exam illustrate the distinction between 'causes' and 'justifications'.

_____

_____

_____

_____

_____

Causal criteria in experiments

The following diagram illustrates the classical experimental design.

	Pre-test measurement	Intervention	Post-test measurement
Experimental group	E1	Yes	E2
Control group	C1	No	C2

Imagine that a researcher decides to use this research design to investigate the effects of eating chocolate (the independent variable) on university students' happiness (the dependent variable). She randomly selects and randomly assigns 20 first-year sociology students between the experimental and control groups. Her measurement of the dependent variable is a self-reported measure of happiness on a 10-point scale. Her measurement of the independent variable is the consumption of an entire chocolate bar.

With respect to this particular experimental design, answer the following questions:

What observations or comparisons would the researcher make to measure changes in the *dependent* variable? *Justify* your answer.

Observations/comparisons: _____

_____

_____

Justification: _____

_____

_____

What observations or comparisons would the researcher make to measure changes in the *independent* variable? *Justify* your answer.

Observations/comparisons: _____

_____

_____

Justification: _____

_____

_____

What observations or comparisons would the researcher use to measure the causal criterion of *association* (i.e., that changing the independent variable is connected to a systematic change in the dependent variable)? *Justify* your answer.

Observations/comparisons: _____

_____

_____

Justification: _____

_____

_____

What observations or comparisons would the researcher use to measure the causal criterion of *sequence* (i.e., ensuring that changes in the independent variable occur prior to observed changes in the dependent variable)? *Justify* your answer.

Observations/comparisons: _____

_____

_____

Justification: _____

_____

_____

What observations or comparisons would the researcher use to ensure that the causal criterion of *non-spuriousness* is met? *Justify* your answer.

Observations/comparisons: _____

_____

_____

Justification: _____

_____

_____

Natural experiments: Twin study logic

There is an ongoing debate in both the natural and social sciences about whether a certain outcome (e.g., alcoholism, schizophrenia, achievement motivation) is the result of biological factors (nature) or socialization influences (nurture). The conventional methodology for inquiring about the relative contributions of nature and nurture is a 'twin study'.

The logic of twin studies is based on the ability to control and vary both genetic heritage and environmental influence. The basic set-up is as follows. On the genetic side, twins come in two basic varieties, identical and fraternal. Identical twins (monozygotic) come from a single egg and therefore have identical DNA. By contrast, fraternal twins (dizygotic) have no greater shared genetic material than other siblings (50 per cent). On the environmental side, twins can be either reared together (in the same family) or reared apart (in different families—through adoption, for example). Another comparison group used in twin studies is randomly selected pairs of people (who share no genetic or environmental heritage).

The following table summarizes several possible types of comparison.

Table 12.1

Environment	Genetics	
	Same (identical twins)	Different (fraternal twins)
Same (reared together)	A	B
Different (reared apart)	C	D

E = randomly selected pairs of people

Imagine that you are interested in using a twin study to examine whether an outcome like 'criminal convictions' is due primarily to nature or to nurture. Explain what kind of conclusions the following scenarios might suggest.

Scenario 1
You only have evidence from cell A—that is, identical twins reared together. If the twins have very similar conviction rates, can you reasonably attribute this to genetic influences? Justify your answer.

_____

_____

_____

Scenario 2

Twins in cell C are found to have much more similar conviction rates than those in group E. What conclusion can you reasonably draw? Justify your answer.

_____

_____

_____

Scenario 3

Twins in cell A are found to have no more similar conviction rates than those in cell B. What conclusion can you reasonably draw? Justify your answer.

_____

_____

_____

Necessity and sufficiency

Necessary conditions are those that must be evident for a particular outcome to occur. Sufficient conditions are those that, when present, are enough to produce a particular outcome.

Imagine that a researcher is interested in the connection between having a 'happy childhood' (the independent variable) and being a 'happy adult'. The researcher conducts a study that includes 200 subjects, divided equally into those who had 'happy' and those who had 'unhappy' childhoods. The following tables present possible outcomes of the research investigation.

Outcome 1

Table 12.2

	Childhood experience	
Adult experience	Happy	Unhappy
Happy	65	0
Unhappy	35	100
	100	100

Outcome 2

Table 12.3

	Childhood experience	
Adult experience	Happy	Unhappy
Happy	100	65
Unhappy	0	35
	100	100

Necessity

Which of these research outcomes indicates that an unhappy childhood is a *necessary condition* for an unhappy adulthood?

_____

With reference to the numbers in the table you selected, provide a *justification* explaining how the evidence demonstrates the criterion of necessity.

_____

_____

_____

_____

_____

Sufficiency

Which of these research outcomes indicates that an unhappy childhood is a *sufficient condition* for an unhappy adulthood?

_____

With reference to the numbers in the table you selected, provide a *justification* explaining how the evidence demonstrates the criterion of sufficiency.

_____

_____

_____

_____

_____

Connections

In the outcome table you selected as demonstrating *necessity*, does the evidence indicate that everyone who experienced an unhappy childhood will become an unhappy adult? Explain your answer with reference to the evidence.

_____

_____

_____

_____

_____

What does the evidence in this table tell you about the *sufficiency* of unhappy childhoods for unhappy adulthoods?

_____

_____

_____

_____

_____

The outcome tables above demonstrate that an independent variable condition can be a necessary contributor to an outcome *or* it can be a sufficient contributor to an outcome.

Now imagine that an unhappy childhood is *both* necessary *and* sufficient for an unhappy adulthood. Put numbers in the following table that would demonstrate the necessary and sufficient condition connecting unhappy childhoods and adulthoods.

Outcome 3

Table 12.4

	Childhood experience	
Adult experience	Happy	Unhappy
Happy		
Unhappy		
	100	100

Explain how the evidence you have entered in this table:

i. Demonstrates necessity

_____

_____

_____

_____

_____

ii. Demonstrates sufficiency

_____

_____

_____

_____

_____

Some scenarios

Read each of the following scenarios and address the causal issue(s) identified.

Scenario 1

A survey researcher completes a study that shows a strong correlation between the variables 'dropping out of high school' and 'drug abuse'. Based on this evidence, is the researcher justified in concluding that dropping out of high school causes drug abuse? Justify your answer.

_____

_____

_____

_____

_____

Scenario 2

A researcher interviews individuals leaving a theatre and asks whether the movie they watched (*The Godfather*) caused a change in their attitudes toward Italians. Explain why this approach does not qualify as a classic experimental design and what changes would be required to make it qualify.

_____

_____

_____

_____

_____

Scenario 3

Here is a description of an experimental study: Researchers wanted to determine whether students were more relaxed after a short period of rest in which classical music was playing compared to a rest period without music. The experimental group was comprised of the first 20 students who arrived at the research room. The next 20 students who arrived comprised the control group. Upon arrival, members of both groups wore a wrist band for five minutes that measured their skin temperature, since skin temperature is lower during times of stress. After this measurement of relaxation, the experimental and control groups were assigned to separate rooms for 20 minutes. During this period, the experimental group heard classical music, while the control group did not. Following the rest period, both groups of students were asked to assess their level of relaxation on a 10-point scale, with higher scores indicating greater relaxation. During the rest period, rock and roll music could be heard from a car radio on the street. As well, three students in the control group used the bathroom during the rest period. At the end of the experiment, the researchers concluded that classical music during a rest period does not increase relaxation, since the two groups had equivalent final relaxation scores.

Is the researchers' conclusion a valid one? If not, what sources of internal invalidity might have confounded their conclusion?

_____

_____

_____

_____

_____

Note: Remember to consult the 'Tips for lab applications' section on the companion website (www.oupcanada.com/methodscoach) if you find you need help.

Notes

'You Play the Way You Practise': A Preface for Students

[1]The labs cover topics from both the 'quantitative' and the 'qualitative' traditions. However, both traditions include many more topics and techniques than are contained in the labs.

[2]As contrasted against the all-too-prevalent disingenuous forms.

Lab 1

[1]Sociology offers a rich variety of theoretical options to choose among. The three theories highlighted here are illustrations only and by no means definitive. But for our present purpose, the challenge would be the same no matter what theoretical alternative was selected. If the goal of a theory is to explain existing conditions and/or anticipate future conditions, then testing the theory requires translating its abstract ideas into a researchable form that is connected to some concrete realities.

[2]R.J. Brym, J. Lie, A. Nelson, N. Guppy, and C. McCormick. 2003. *Sociology: Your Compass for a New World*. 1st Canadian edn, p. 167. Toronto: Thomson Nelson. © 2005 Nelson Education Ltd. Reproduced by permission. www.cengage.com/permissions.

[3]Ibid., p. 168.

[4]Ibid., p. 166.

Lab 2

[1]From Peter C. Newman's review of Jean Chrétien's *My Years as Prime Minister* (Toronto: Knopf Canada), *The Globe and Mail*, 20 October 2007, p. D6.

[2]The fact that it was the *white* suicide rate only is not important for our purposes here.

[3]Steven Stack and Jim Gundlach. 1992. 'The effect of country music on suicide'. *Social Forces* 71: 211–18.

[4]Found in Gwynne Nettler. 1970. *Explanations*, p. 71. Toronto: McGraw-Hill.

[5]These well-known examples are reported in Rodney Stark and Lynne Roberts. 1996. *Contemporary Research Methods*, p. 8–9. Bellevue, WA: MicroCase Corporation.

Lab 3

[1]In Alice's fantastic world, Humpty Dumpty scornfully declares that 'When I use a word, it means just what I choose it to mean—neither more nor less.'

[2]World Health Organization. *Preamble to the Constitution of the World Health Organization*, as adopted by the International Health Conference, New York, 19–22 June 1946; signed on 22 July 1946 by the representatives of 61 states (Official Records of the World Health Organization, no. 2, p. 100), and entered into force on 7 April 1948.

[3]Note that each of these concepts presents its own further dilemmas. For example, how do we define 'homeless'? Living in a car for two days? Living under a bridge? Does living in a shelter count as homelessness? Conceptualization is a process that tends to involve the continual refinement of definitions.

[4]Philip Giles. 2004. *Low Income Measurement in Canada*. Ottawa: Statistics Canada. Catalogue no. 75F0002MIE, p. 6.

[5]Ibid., p. 7.

[6]Robert J. Brym and John Lie. 2005. *Sociology: Your Compass for a New World*, p. 382. Toronto: Nelson.

[7]Arthur G. Neal and Melvin Seeman. 1964. 'Organizations and powerlessness: A test of the mediation hypothesis'. *American Sociological Review* 29: 216–26.

Lab 4

[1]There is one exception to this rule, which involves cases in which too much precision can make a question seem threatening. A question about the variable 'income', for example, could be measured at a high level by asking respondents to report income to the nearest dollar. This would be imprudent, however, because it would increase respondent resistance.

[2]Note that in most cases, these are merely examples of attributes for each variable rather than an exhaustive list.

Lab 5

[1]One useful elaboration of this law can be found in Anthony L. Haynor's (2003) *Social Practice: Philosophy and Method* (Kendall/Hunt Publishing Company).

[2]In his wonderful little book *Tricks of the Trade* (1998), Howard S. Becker, the stellar qualitative researcher, captures this point in a section entitled 'Random sampling: A perfect solution (for some problems)', p. 68 (University of Chicago Press).

[3]Examples of such qualitative studies include: Niels Braroe. 1975. *Indian and White: Self Image and Interaction in a Canadian Plains Community* (Stanford University Press); Carolyn Ellis. 1986. Fisher Folk: *Two Communities on Chesapeake Bay* (University of Kentucky Press); John Lofland and Rodney Stark. 1965. 'Becoming a world-saver: A theory of conversion to a deviant perspective'. *American Sociological Review* 30: 862–75.

[4]Michael Patton, the renowned evaluation researcher, lists 16 types in one of his books (*Qualitative Research and Evaluation Methods*. 2001. Sage Publications).

Lab 6

[1]Howard Schuman. 2002. 'Sense and nonsense about surveys'. *Contexts* 1 (2): 40–7.

[2]Note: The term 'harm reduction' describes 'a concept aiming to prevent or reduce negative consequences associated with certain behaviours', mainly the spread of diseases like HIV and Hepatitis C and overdose deaths due to injecting drug use. Specific harm reduction strategies include needle exchange programs and drug substitutes like methadone maintenance. Public health advocates of this approach believe that public policy should treat addicts as ill rather than criminal. (Source: World Health Organization. www.who.int/hiv/topics/harm/reduction/en. Accessed 8 September 2005). In 2003, Vancouver opened Insite, North America's first government-sanctioned and supervised safe injection site.

Lab 11

[1]Statistics Canada. *Vital Statistics Compendium 1996*. Catalogue no. 84-214-XPE.

[2]H.W. Hoek. 2006. 'Incidence, prevalence, and mortality of anorexia nervosa and other eating disorders'. *Current Opinion in Psychiatry* 19 (4): 389–94.

About the Authors

Lance W. Roberts is a Professor in the Sociology Department and a Fellow of St. John's College at the University of Manitoba. He recently completed a term as Scientific Director of the Winnipeg Area Study, a survey research unit. For more than three decades, he has taught undergraduate and graduate methods and statistics courses and is the author of several books and dozens of articles on topics related to social trends, ethnic relations, education, and inequality.

Karen Kampen is a Doctoral Candidate in the Sociology Department's PhD program at the University of Manitoba, where she holds the position of Lab Instructor. Her main areas of interest are environmental sociology and research methods. She has spent 15 years working in universities as a Research Associate, collecting and analyzing data for long-term projects such as a health care program evaluation and books on social trends and poverty. She also serves as an Instructor for introductory sociology and undergraduate methods courses.

Tracey Peter is an Assistant Professor in the Sociology Department at the University of Manitoba. Her areas of specialization include data analysis and syntax programming, skills she advanced during her tenure as a Research Associate and Programming Manager with a nationally based evaluation research company. Professor Peter currently teaches undergraduate and graduate courses in research methods and statistics and is working on several projects in mental health and violence, suicide prevention, education, and immigration research.

Index

Page numbers in **bold** refer to lab application exercises.